A HAND-BOOK FOR VISITORS TO DEHLI AND ITS NEIGHBOURHOOD

A HAND-BOOK FOR VISITORS TO DEHLI AND ITS NEIGHBOURHOOD

H. G. KEENE, M.R.A.S.

Fourth Edition

GYAN

Published by

Gyan Publishing House
5, Ansari Road
Daryaganj, New Delhi-110002
Phone: 011-47034999, 9811692060
E-mail: books@gyanbooks.com

Distribution Network
gyanbooks.com
India, USA, Canada, UK, Australia, France

ISBN : 978-81-212-9675-5 (PB)
Fourth Edition Published, 1882

Fifth Impression 2023

Printed at: Gyan Press, Delhi.

A HAND-BOOK FOR VISITORS TO DEHLI AND ITS NEIGHBOURHOOD
Author: H. G. KEENE

A

HAND-BOOK FOR VISITORS

TO

DEHLI

AND ITS NEIGHBOURHOOD.

BY

H. G. KEENE, M.R.A.S.,

AUTHOR OF "THE TURKS IN INDIA;" "HAND-BOOK FOR VISITORS TO AGRA," &c.

FOURTH EDITION.

1882.

ADVERTISEMENT TO THE FOURTH EDITION.

The favour with which the former editions have been received by the public has led to the preparation of the present issue. Errors have been corrected, additions made, and a more accurate system of transliteration adopted. It is hoped that, by these means, the work may be enabled to retain its acceptance, and that its usefulness may be increased. The plans are reprinted from General Cunningham's Archæological Report. For detailed information, the reader may be referred to the elaborate work of Mr. Carr-Stephen, *the Archæology of Dehli.*

NOTICE.

The following system of spelling, adopted by the Government of India, will be pursued throughout this book. It is, however, to be borne in mind that it is only *an approximation*, especially as to consonants, which, in many instances, cannot be correctly transliterated in English.

a, as 1st (a) in "afar."

á, as 2nd (a) in "afar."

e, as (e) in "they."

i, as 2nd (i) in "quinine."

u, as (u) in "bull," or "rule."

Consonants require no further explanation.

[It may help the reader to remember that these sounds are expressed by the vowels in the English words "ruminant" and "obey;" excepting when they are accented, indicating a broader pronunciation.]

CONTENTS.

—:o:—

APPENDICES.

GUIDE TO DEHLI.

INTRODUCTION.

The station of Dehli is reached by a short siding of the East India Railway from the terminus at Gháziabád Junction, which, crossing the Jamná by a fine girder-bridge, and passing through the old Fort of *Salimgarh* and a corner of Sháhjahán's "Red Castle," or *Lál Killá*, lands the traveller in the neighbourhood of the *Queen's Gardens*. He will find several Hotels advertised, but the *personnel*, and therefore the administration, of Indian Hotels is always changing. There is also a Government *Dák Bangálow*, which is well kept, and centrally situated.

At all these houses there is likely to be a guide acquainted, more or less, with the English language; but it is hoped that readers of this work will have but little occasion for their services.

Dehli, the Rome of Asia, consists, besides the modern city, of ruins spreading over a length of ten miles by a breadth averaging little less than six. In this area are comprised the traditional "seven castles and fifty-two gates" spoken of as far back as 1611 by the merchant Finch. To the North is the new city of Sháhjahán, which was not built in Finch's time. In order to form any idea of the contents of so thickly-covered a space as this is, some method must be adopted; and perhaps Captain Harcourt's Diary* will be found most useful for the purpose by those who have but a short time to devote to the subject. Those whose leisure is more ample may still avail themselves of the Diary, by pursuing the same order of work, but doing less each day. If only two days can be spared, the best plan will probably be to give the first to the modern city, and the second to a drive to the Kutab and return by Humáyun's tomb and Ferozábád.

"*1st day.*—The Jamá Masjid.

---

* New Guide to Dehli. Meerut, 1870. I would once for all acknowledge my constant obligations to this the first serious attempt to do justice to Dehli.

"The Fort, including the Dewán Ám, the Dewán Kháss, the King's Bath and Pearl Mosque (Note.—Drive to the Dewán Kháss, the guide there will show all that is to be seen —a trifle may be given to him, say 4 annas); the Kálán Masjid near the Tarcomán Gate of the city, but this is only interesting to antiquarians.

"*2nd day.*—Drive out by the Dehli Gate of the city, and *en passant* look at Feroz Sháh's Lát, or Stone Pillar, and the views of the city of Ferozábád just outside the gate to the left of the road; go on to Humáyun's Tomb, and while there visit Nizamuddin's Tomb (a fee of 4 annas for each person is generally given), the Chausat Kambá, and the other ruined Mosques, &c., adjacent. On the way back leave the carriage outside the Fort of Purána Killá, and walk (about half a mile) to Sher Sháh's Mosque, which is well worth seeing.

"*3rd day.*—Drive towards the Kutab, passing the ruins of the Janter Manter, or Observatory, on the left, and Safter Jang's Mausoleum on the right, both well worth seeing. The various tombs and galleries at the Kutab will employ the rest of the day. In the evening, walk round the top of the wall of Lalkat Fort to the left of the Minár; ladies could hardly manage this, as the pathway is composed, on the west and most interesting and best preserved side, of large loose stones. Sleep at the Kutab Dák Bangálow.

"*4th day.*—Go to Mausoleum of Sultán Gári; the chaprássie of the Bangálow can give every information. In the evening drive to Tuglackábád, three miles from Kutab, visit the ruined city and the tomb of Tuglack Sháh, return to Kutab, and next morning come back to Dehli."

A few words will suffice as to the early history of the neighbourhood. Tradition claims it as a settlement of the early Aryans, whose history is supposed to be imbedded in the mythical epic called *Máhábháráta*. (*Vide infra*, p. 29.) The seat of Hindu monarchy, however, if it was here in those remote days, was removed before the Christian era, when the great power in Upper India was that of the Buddhist King, or Emperor, of Palibothra. The history of Dehli remains very obscure till the 8th century A.D. when it became a metropolis of the Tamar Rajpoots (*vide infra*, p. 44), whose overthrow by the Patháns of Ghazni led to the formation of the first empire of the Mahomedans in India, A.D. 1193. When the Patháns became engaged with the early Tartar invaders the cities of this plain were united for purposes of fortification and defence. In the decline of the Pathán empire a good deal of the business of war and peace came to be transferred to the eastern parts of Hindustan. Bábar found the Lodi ruler established at Agra, and there he himself settled and died (*vide infra*, p. 67 and *The Agra Guide*).

Humáyun towards the end of his troubled life, settled at Dehli, where he died (*infra*, p. 31), and the city was immediately seized in the interest of Sháh Adil, his Afghán rival. On Akbar's overthrowing the latter, the seat of Government was once more removed to Agra; which is therefore almost exclusively a Moghul city, and which continued to be the capital of the empire till Sháhjahán removed, for a time at least, to the modern city of Dehli, which he built and called by his own name, Shájahánábád. It thus comes to pass that Dehli—understanding by the term the parallelogram above referred to—is more interesting than Agra, if less beautiful. The very monarch who last chose it as a capital dowered the forsaken rival with a treasure which, as it is unique in the world, is quite unapproached by anything at Dehli. But if the latter has no Táj, it offers to the visitor interested in ethnology, in history, and in architecture, a series of records that may almost be compared to the stratified annals of geology.* With harder work and less enjoyment than in Agra, the visitor to Dehli will nevertheless find his mind interested, and his knowledge of men and their works sensibly increased.

Lying on the bank of the Jamná, and in a basin receiving the drainage of the Mewát Hills, the neighbourhood is well-watered, and sheltered from storms. Its commercial advantages are scarcely on a par with those of Agra; but it is better situated in some other respects—nearer to the hills for purposes of pleasure, nearer to the frontier for purposes of defence, and enjoying a somewhat milder climate. Nevertheless after the death of Humáyun in A.D. 1556, which resulted from an accident at the *Sher Mandal* in the fortified city of his late rival, now known as *Puráná Killá*.† Dehli, as just shown, ceased to attract any share of imperial favour for nearly eighty years. During the long reign of Akbar, and during that of his son, Agra and Lahore‡ formed the chief seats of Government; but in 1635 A.D., just before setting out on his second Deccan expedition, Sháhjahán ordered the construction of a totally new city to the north of that inhabited by his great-grandfather. It

* The reader is referred to the Architectural Notes in the Appendix to the 1st part of this series (Agra).

† *Vide infra*, p. 31.

‡ So thought Milton;—"Agra and Lahore of Great Mogul."

is possible that Agra had become distasteful to the Emperor since it had become the burial-place of the wife of his youth—the lady of the Táj, or that mere caprice and the desire to spend money largely in the gratification of a favourite taste may have actuated him or both. The following is Bernier's account, who saw the new works in their first freshness, having landed in India in 1665:

"It is now about forty years," Bernier was writing after he had been nearly nine years in the country, "that Sháh Jahán, father of the Grand-Moghal *Aureng-Zebe*, now reigning, to eternize his memory, caused to be built a town contiguous to old *Dehli*, which he called after his name, *Sháh-Jahán-Abád*, and, by way of abbreviation, *Jehán-Abád*, that is to say, a colony of *Cháh-Jehán*, designing to make it the capital of the Empire, instead of *Agra*, where he said that the summer heats were too violent. This nearness hath occasioned, that the ruins of old *Dehli* have served to build a new city; and in the Indies they scarce speak any more of *Dehli*, but only *Jehán-Abád*. Yet, notwithstanding since the City of *Jehán-Abád* is not yet known amongst us, I intend to speak of it under the old name of *Dehli*, which is familiar to us."

The works were probably supervised by Ali-Mardán Khán, the Persian adventurer who joined Sháhjahán's service in 1637. He made the canal, which still supplies the neighbourhood with water, and was probably the introducer of the bulbous dome which forms so marked a note in the decadence of Saracenic architecture in India. The Táj,—which is the earliest specimen of this fault with which I am acquainted,—was designed two years after the arrival of Ali-Mardán in India: the Jamá Masjid of Agra, built a year or two earlier, has a dome which, without being by any means flat, is yet bold and almost natural.

THE FORT AND PALACE OF THE MUGHALS.

This fortress of New Dehli was built at an expense of no more than fifty lakhs of the money of that day, according to the *Mirat-i-Aftábnamá*, and was twenty years in progress. It is about 1¼ mile in circumference, and within it were contained originally about a dozen principal buildings, of which some have perished, but the most important still exist in good preservation. A ground plan of the palace as it was will be found in Fergusson's *Indian Architecture*; also in Mr. Carr-Stephen's book. There are on the city side two entrances, which are both much in the same state as when Bernier saw them a few years after their completion. After describing these entries, the one guarded by the two statues of the defenders of Chittor,* the other made through the mighty bastion of the Lahore Gate, still standing, the French traveller in his usual lively manner detains us for a moment at the *Naubakthánd*, or "Nagar-kanay," as he calls it, and tells us how by use, and living at a distance, he had learned to find "something majestical" in a "Musick" that was at first "insufferable" to him. He then proceeds to describe the Royal Halls as he saw them in their pristine splendour:—

"Over against the great gate of the Court, upon which is the *Nagar-kanay*, beyond the whole Court, there is a great and stately hall, with many ranks of pillars high raised, very airy, open on three sides, looking to the Court, and having its pillars and ground painted and guilded. In the midst of the wall, which separated this hall from the *Seraglio*, there is an opening, or a kind of great window high and large, and so high that a man cannot reach to it from below with his hand. There it is where the King appears seated upon his throne, having his sons on his sides, and some eunuchs standing, some of which drive away the flies with peacock's tails, others fan him with great fans, others stand there ready with great respect and humility for several services. Thence he seeth beneath him all the *Umráhs*, *Rájás*, and Ambassadors, who are also all of them standing upon a raised ground encompassed with silver rails, with their eyes downwards, and their hands crossing their stomachs: somewhat further off he seeth the *Mán-sebdárs*, or lesser Umráhs, which are also all standing in the same posture and respect as the Umráhs do: and somewhat further off, in the remaining part of the hall, and in the Court, he seeth a great crowd of all sorts of people. For there it is where the King, every day about noon, giveth a general audience to all; which is the reason that this great hall is called *Ám-Khás*, that is, place of audience, or a place of meeting common to great and small."

We are then entertained with a description of the parade of elephants and fighting animals, and next told how "often also one or two of the Umráhs cause at that time to pass their cavalry for a review before the King: the Umráhs coveting

* *Vide* Appendix A.

that their horsemen should appear gallant, advantageously decked with extraordinary garments, and their horses trapped with iron, and harnessed with I know not how many different and odd fashions.

"Feats of arms are exhibited by the younger lords; and the amusements come to an end. Meantime all these divertisements are nothing but an interlude of serious affairs; for as I have said, the King omits not to make a muster of his cavalry, and well to view them himself. We have seen that the war being ended, there is not one cavalier, nor any other soldier, but he hath seen him and examined him, either to increase his pay, or to lessen it, or quite to cashier him. Besides it is seen every day, that he commands the petitions, which are showed him afar off in the crowd of the people, to be brought to him and to be read: ordering the parties concerned to approach, and examining them and often causing justice to be done them immediately, although he hath the *Addlet-kánáy*, the Chamber of Justice, where he, ordinarily, is present once a week, attended by his two first *Kádys*, or Chief Justices: and though also at one other time in the week he hath the patience to hear in private, for the space of two hours, ten persons of the common people, whom a good and rich old man presents to him. Whence it appears (to note that by the by) that those Kings, how barbarous soever esteemed by us, do yet constantly remember that they owe justice to their subjects."

Passing from the *Ám-Khás*—a name given at that time both to the Dewán-Ám and to the space in front—the traveller proceeds to conduct us to what is now called the *Dewán-Khás*, but which Bernier calls the *Goselhkáné*,* that is, the place to wash in. "But few are suffered to enter there; neither is the court of it so great as that of the *Ám-Khás*: but the hall is very handsome, spacious, painted and guilded, and its floor raised four or five foot high. There it is where the King is seated in a chair, his Umráhs standing round about him, and giveth a more particular audience to his Officers, receiveth their Accompts, and treateth of the most important affairs of state. All the Umráhs are obliged to be without fail every evening at this assembly, as in the morning at the *Ám-Khás*; else something is retrenched of their pay."

The great gateway of the *Naubatkháná*, or "Music-house," opened, as we have seen, on the *Díwán-i-Ám*, which (as at

* It appears from contemporary writers that this was the name usually given to the more private apartments in a Mogul palace.

Agra) formed the main frontage of the Palace. Like that of Agra, it is, on three sides, an open stone tabernacle, raised on slender shafts and wavy arches, of which the red stone surface (now bare) was once covered with ornamental plaster. And the fourth side (towards the private apartments) is, as at Agra, a wall. In the midst of this, and raised about ten feet from the floor, was Bernier's "window" containing the throne reached from behind by a staircase leading from the private apartments, to be more particularly described presently. This throne was placed in a sort of alcove, the front of which was covered over with a kind of *baldochino* or pavilion in white marble with gilt mouldings: the back and sides of the above were inlaid somewhat in the fashion of the buildings of Sháh-jahán at Agra, but the inlay on the back wall was originally remarkable for the introduction, at certain distances, of frames containing pictures of birds and animals, and of fruits and flowers, treated with an attempt at realism, in no degree resembling the usual art-practice of the Massalmáns, and more like Italian *pietra dura*. The description that follows is from Beresford's *Delhi*, a work published just before the mutiny by the then manager of the Dehli Bank, who was one of the victims to popular fury on that melancholy occasion:

"It is a large hall, open at three sides, and supported by rows of red sandstone pillars, formerly adorned with gilding and stucco work. In the wall at the back is a staircase that leads up to the throne, which is raised about ten feet from the ground, and is covered by a canopy supported on four pillars of white marble, the whole being curiously inlaid with mosaic work; behind the throne is a doorway by which the Emperor entered from his private apartments. The whole of the wall behind the throne is covered with mosaic *paintings*, in precious stones of the most beautiful flowers, fruits, birds, and beasts of Hindustan. Most of them are represented in a very natural manner. They were executed by Austin de Bordeaux,* who, after defrauding several of the Princes of Europe by means of false gems which he fabricated with great skill, sought refuge at the Court of Sháh Jehán, where he made his fortune, and was in high favour with the Emperor. In front of the throne, and slightly raised above the floor of the hall, is a large slab of white marble, which was formerly richly inlaid with mosaic works, of which the traces only now remain."—*Beresford's Delhi*, 1856.

* Information about this artist will be found in the work on Agra already referred to [*Vide* especially, p. 122, for Bernier's description of the Moghul Court.]

A native artist has done his best to restore this work in lac; but the figure of the old French designer, "a long-haired Orpheus fiddling among the animals," is no longer to be observed. It was the representation of a beardless youth, with flowing yellow locks, seated upon a rock beneath a tree with a leopard, a hare, and a lion crouching at his feet—all in the Italian taste of the day. It is said that these pieces of inlay were plundered by a military officer at the siege in 1857, and made up into tables, etc., by him. These he afterwards sold to the Home Government for £500. The inlaid portrait of Austin de Bordeaux is now in the Museum of the India Office in London.

Proceeding towards the left, the Hall of Special Audience, or *House of Lords*, is reached; a smaller hall, in echelon, to the first, raised on a marble *estrade*, about four feet high, with a small but chastely carved balustrade of perforated marble on the front side. The columns of this, the finest hall of its kind in India, are inlaid below with precious stones in floral designs, the upper sections, as well as the ceiling and cornices, being very tastefully gilt. In an old work taken from Mandelslo, Thevenot, and other travellers, it is thus described:—"Two and thirty marble columns sustain as many arches; and these columns are about four feet square with their base and mouldings. When the Emperor Chá Jehán caused that hall to be built, he ordered that it should be all enriched with the finest work of inlaid jewels, like the great duke's chapel in Italy."* "But when they had made the trial on some column to the height of two or three feet, they saw it would be impossible to find a number of jewels sufficient to execute such a grand design, and that the expense would amount to immense sums. They were therefore obliged to abandon that project." Then follows a description of the famous Peacock Throne, valued by Tavernier (himself a jeweller) at "two hundred millions of livres." A better description is that extracted below from Beresford's *Delhi*. The white marble platform on which this extraordinary piece of extravagance rested is still in the hall; and on the cornices at each end is still to be decyphered the famous inscription, in the most beautiful flowing Persian characters, raised and gilt, "*Agar furduse baru-i-zamin ast, hamin ast, hamin ast, hamin ast*"—familiar to readers of *Lalla Rookh* as—"If there be an elysium on earth, it is this, it is this, it is this."

* The Medicean Chapel at Florence, *vide* Agra Handbook, Appendix A,—"Stone Industries of Agra."

"In this hall was the famous Peacock Throne, so called from its having the figures of two peacocks standing behind it, their tails being expanded, and the whole so inlaid with sapphires, rubies, emeralds, pearls, and other precious stones of appropriate colours as to represent life. The throne itself was six feet long by four feet broad; it stood on six massive feet, which, with the body, were of solid gold, inlaid with rubies, emeralds, and diamonds. It was surmounted by a canopy of gold, supported by twelve pillars, all richly emblazoned with costly gems, and a fringe of pearls ornamented the borders of the canopy. Between the two peacocks stood the figure of a parrot of the ordinary size, said to have been carved out of a single emerald (?). On either side of the throne stood an umbrella, one of the oriental emblems of royalty; they were formed of crimson velvet, richly embroidered and fringed with pearls,—the handles were eight feet high, of solid gold, and studded with diamonds. The cost of this superb work of art has been variously stated at sums varying from one to six millions of pounds sterling. It was planned and executed under the supervision of Austin de Bordeaux, already mentioned as the artist who executed the mosaic work in the Ám-khás."—*Beresford's Delhi.*

There is nothing left now of the Peacock Throne, but there used to be a model of it in the Imámbára at Lucknow, which, like so much else that was curious and valuable, perished in the troubles of Fifty-seven. It would appear that this costly piece of ostentation, valued by the jeweller Tavernier at so large a sum, was not remarkable for grace of design; being merely a sort of large four-post bed, with two peacocks and a parrot perched upon the tester, but all of gems and gold.

The ceiling of the Dewán Khás, in which this throne stood, was plated with solid silver. But the throne itself was broken up and plundered by Nádir Sháh in 1739, and the plating torn down by the Máhráttás in 1760, when they occupied the city for a few months prior to their frightful slaughter by the Afghâns at Pánipat.*

Turning to the left we enter the Hammám, or Turkish Bath, once beautifully inlaid, and now very creditably restored. At the back is the royal Mosque, an elegant structure of white marble, smaller than that in the Agra Palace, but more ornamented. On the opposite, or south side of the Dewán-i-Khás, some of the buildings have been removed (though their foundations can still be traced). But the *Khás Mahal* and *Rang*

* *Vide* Keene's *Fall of the Moghul Empire*, p. 61.

Mahal still remain, and suffice to show the sumptuous, though not extensive, style of Sháhjahán's private life. In the middle of the tracery screen between the Dewán-i-Khás and the private rooms is the symbol of a pair of scales in colours and gold. The *Khás Mahal* is an exquisite suite of apartments, resembling in style the rooms now occupied by the Museum of the Archæological Society at Agra, but with a greater display of wall-painting and decoration than those rooms ever boasted. The name is given to the rooms contained in the *Samman Burj*, or "Jasmine Bastion," devoted to the Monarch's retirement: and all are a marvel of white marble with floral colouring. The *Rang Mahal* beyond is now used as a Mess-house. All the cupolas of this suite were formerly covered with gilt copper.

Between the palace and the bridge is an older fort, the Salimgarh, built by the son of Sher Sháh, the interrex of Humáyun, and only now noticeable as being the only building of importance in that neighbourhood before the site was selected by Sháhjahán. This small fort is not possessed of much beauty or interest; but is curious as having been used as the 'Tower' or state-prison of the Moghuls. The island on which it stands was connected with the shore by a bridge of five arches by Jahángir—one of the few things he ever did for Dehli.

The palace of Sháhjahánábád, in the short space of its existence, has witnessed many startling scenes, mostly tragic. Here, in 1716, the Scottish Surgeon, who cured the Emperor Farrokh Siyar on the eve of his marriage, was rewarded by that permission for his employers to establish a factory, and to maintain a territory of thirty-eight towns on the Banks of the Hooghly, which was the foundation of the "Presidency of Fort William," and all that has since sprung therefrom. Gabriel Hamilton was thus the *homme nécessaire* of the British Indian Empire. Here, on the 31st March, 1739, the degenerate Mahamad Sháh entered the Throne-room with the fearful Nádir Sháh of Persia, and sipped his coffee on the Peacock Throne. Next day the invaders massacred the citizens before "the dark and terrible eye" of their leader as he looked on from the roof of Roshun-ud-dowláh's Mosque.

The Peacock Throne was then broken up, and Nádir returned to Persia with plunder valued at eighty millions sterling in the value of the day. Less than ten years after the Abdáli Chief of Cábul, Ahmad Khán, repeated the cruel lesson, and despoiled the Palace of much of its remaining wealth. In 1759 the work was completed by the Máhráttás, under Sadásheo Ráo Bháo, marching to their ruin at Pánipat; when, as before mentioned, the plating was torn down from the ceiling of the Throne-room. In 1788 the sanctity of the imperial halls was further violated by the cannon-shot of Gholám Kádir, and shortly after by his actual presence. Here he lay and smoked his *hukáh* on the faded substitute of the Peacock Throne; and here he, with his own hands, shared in the torture of the royal family and the blinding of the helpless old Emperor Sháh Álam. Here on the 15th September, 1803, as the sun was setting, the long cavalcade of Lake defiled into the Ám-Khás, where the blinded chief of the house of Timur was found "seated under a small tattered canopy, the remnant of his Royal State, with every external appearance of the misery of his condition." And lastly, here, in May, 1857, the last representative of the Great Moghuls, a not unwilling tool in the hands of the Company's mutinous soldiery, consented to the butchery of helpless women and children.

The original ground-plan of the Palace, beginning from the northward, embraced (1) the *Burj-i-Shamáli*, a raised pavilion of white marble, containing the marble bath inlaid with precious stones; (2) the waterworks and garden; (3) the *Dewán-Khás*, already described, opening out of the private apartments reserved for the Emperor's own use, all richly incrusted with patterns and inscriptions; (4) the block of residences called *Imtiáz Mahal*, once splendid with gilding and *pietra dura*, enclosing a garden about 300 feet square, with abundant fountains; (5) west of this stood the *Dewán-Ám*, still extant in much of its original beauty of carved sandstone and decorated marble; this formed the public facade of the Palace, opening, as before stated, on the *Naubatkhánó*, or music-gate, and forming a sort of *aula regis* for the disposal of business in the sight of the public. For an account of the inner life of the Palace in the last days of the Court, see Mr. Parkes's *Wanderings of a Pilgrim* (Richardson, London, 1850). A curious book with much miscellaneous information, trustworthy whenever it is *direct*.

Fergusson, who saw these things before the mutiny, says:—"Its principal entrance is from the Chándni Chouk, a splendid wide street, nearly a mile long, planted with two rows of trees and with a canal* of water flowing down its centre. Entering within the deeply-recessed portal you find yourself beneath the roof a vaulted hall, similar in plan to a Gothic Cathedral,

* This canal has been since covered in with masonry.

many of which it excels in dimensions. In the centre it is crossed by another hall at right angles, leading to the lateral Courts, and at the upper end is the great Court of the Palace . . . . the whole forms perhaps the most noble entrance to a Palace known to exist anywhere." After describing briefly the two halls, on the second of which he bestows warm commendation, the writer proceeds :—"To the left are the gardens laid out in the formal style of the East; and the little golden Mosque, an elaborate and beautiful piece of art, but far too small for such a Palace . . . . on the other side is the harem Court, to which no European is admitted . . . . Along the river front, as at Agra, are a number of marble pavilions, generally octagon, covered with gilded domes, some of them of great beauty." So it was in 1857. But since the mutiny most of these buildings have been swept away, or immured in British military constructions.

JAMA' MASJID.

The great Mosque of Sháhjahán is the next object that demands the attention of the visitor. The following is the just and picturesque description of Bernier :—

"The great *Mosque*, seen afar off in the midst of the town, standing upon a rock, flatted to build upon, and to make round about a large place for four long and fair streets to end upon, and answering to the four sides of the Mosquee, *viz.*, one to the principal gate, or frontispiece, another behind that, and the two others to the two gates that are in the middle of the two remaining sides. To come to the gates, there are twenty-five or thirty steps of fair and large stones going round about, except the back-part, which is covered with other great quarry-stones to cover the unevenness of the cut rock; which contributes much to make this fabrick make a shew. The three entries are stately; there is nothing but marble, and their large gates are covered with copper plates exceedingly well wrought. Above the principal gate, which is much statelier than the two others, there are many small turrets of white marble as well without as within; that in the middle is much bigger and higher than the two others. All the rest of the Mosquee, I mean from these three domes unto the great gate, is without covering, because of the heat of the country; and the whole pavement is of large squares of marble. I grant willingly that this structure is not according to the rules and orders of Architecture, which we esteem is indispensably to be followed; yet I observe nothing in it that offends the eye; but rather find all to be well contrived, and well proportioned."

As for the uses of this magnificent temple, take the following further extract:—

"This Mosquee it is to which the King repaireth every Friday (which is the Sunday of the Mahametans) to pay his devotion. Before he goes out of the fortress, the streets he is to pass are constantly watered, because of the heat and dust. Two or three hundred musquetiers are to stand and make a lane about the gate of the fortress, and as many more on the sides of a great street that ends at the Mosquee. The King is followed by a body of Umráhs, some of which are on horseback, some in a *Pálekey*. Among these Umráhs there are many *Mán-sebdars* and mace-bearers, such as I have before spoken of. And though this be not that splendid and magnificent procession, or rather mascarade of the Grand Seignior (I have no proper name for it), nor the warlike order of our Kings, it being altogether of another fashion, yet for all that there is something great and royal in it."

The following is Beresford's account:—

"It has three entrances by handsome gateways of red sandstone, which are approached by magnificent flights of steps of the same material. The principal gateway is to the east side, and is much longer and handsomer than those on the north and south. They all lead into a large quadrangle paved with fine large sandstones, in the centre of which is a marble reservoir of water. On the west side of the square stands the Mosque itself, which is of an oblong form, 201 feet in length and 120 feet broad, and surmounted by three superb cupolas of white marble crowned with culices, or spires of copper richly gilt. The front of the building is partly faced with white marble, and along the cornice are the compartments, each ten feet long and two-and-a-half feet broad, which are inlaid with black marble inscriptions in the Niski character. The interior is paved throughout with slabs of white marble three feet long by one and-a-half broad, each decorated with a black border, which gives it an extremely beautiful appearance. Part of the inner wall is also faced with plain white marble. Near the kibla, or that part which indicates the direction of the city of Mecca, is a handsome Taq, or niche adorned with a profusion of rich friezework, and though joined in several places, appears to have been cut out of a solid block of white marble four feet high and six feet in length. The Mosque is flanked by two minarets 130 feet high, composed of white marble and red sandstone placed vertically in alternate stripes, and access is obtained to the top of them by flights of narrow steps of red sandstone in the interior; at about equal distance there are three projecting galleries, and they are crowned with light pavilions of white marble. . . . Three sides of the terrace, on which this magnificent edifice stands, are enclosed by a colonnade of sandstone, and each corner is ornamented by octagonal pavilions of white marble; the supporting columns being of red sandstone. In the quadrangle at the north-east and south-east are low pillars, on the top of which are fixed marble slabs, on one of which is engraved the Eastern Hemisphere, on the other there are marked certain hour lines; each has an upright iron spike or gnomon, and the shadows shown by the sun indicate to the faithful the time of prayer."—*Beresford's Delhi*, 1856.

This Mosque is a fine specimen of the architecture of Sháhjahán. Like the Mosque in the Agra Tripolya, it has a central dome and two side domes; but it differs from the Agra building, not merely in the vast extent of its quadrangle and the cloisters open to the outside, but also in form and colour. The domes are of pure marble; and, instead of rising at once from the roof-line, are placed upon drums, out of which they imerge in a curve that almost resembles that of a balloon. It was begun in 1644, just seven years later than the Agra Mosque; and it shows signs of the turning-point for the worse which about that time occurs in Hindustani art.* It is said to have employed a daily average of 5,000 workmen for a period of six years, but it was not finally completed till A.D. 1658, the same year that witnessed the deposition of its founder the Emperor Sháhjahán. It stands on a rocky eminence less than a hundred yards to the westward of the Palace Gate; and in later days this short pilgrimage formed the limit of the extramural movements of the once "Great Moghul." Hither, on the *Eed*, the King of Dehli came in faded pomp, and here the sacrifice of Abraham was reproduced by a camel which was slaughtered by the hands of Royalty—here on a Friday in September 1857 was read the last Litany for the house of Timur.

In conclusion, it may be added that Fergusson (*Hist. Archit. II*, 688) takes this Mosque as a type of the religious building of the age, and adds that in all such the eastern gate

* *Vide Agra*, p. 13.

will be found more splendid than those to the north and south, the western extremity being necessarily occupied by the portion expressly set apart for prayer and preaching, and backed by the *Mihráb* or recess looking to Mecca. He says further, "the whole forms a group intelligible at the first glance, and, as an architectural object, possesses a variety of outline and play of light and shade which few buildings can equal."

THE CITY.

The following brief sketch of the City and its contents has been chiefly borrowed from Captain Harcourt:—

"The circuit of the walls of the City is five and-a-half miles: of the citadel and palace one and-a-half miles. The latter has two entrances, called respectively the Lahore and the Dehli Gates.

"The City has ten as below:—

1.—The Calcutta Gate to the N. E., close to the Palace: this leads to the Railway.
2.—The Cashmere Gate to the N., by the Church and Katcherry.
3.—The Moree Gate to the N.
4.—The Cabul Gate to the W., facing the Sudder Bazaar.
5.—The Lahore Gate to the W., faces the Sudder Bazaar, and is the exit from the Chándni Chouk.
6.—The Fárásh Kháná Gate to the S. W.
7.—The Ájmere Gate to the S. W.
8.—The Tarkomán Gate to the S.
9.—The Dehli Gate to the S.
10.—Ráj Ghát to the E., facing the River.

"Entering by the Cashmere Gate, the road to the extreme right leads to the Dehli and Punjab Railway Terminus, on the Hamilton Road. By the road to the left, which may be called the main road of Dehli, the visitor passes the Law Courts and the Church built by Colonel Skinner. Further on he will remark the Government Dehli College, a building with a lofty pillared verandah. Beyond is the Magazine, now used as Dâk Bungalow, Post Office, and Telegraph Office, a portion of which was blown up by Lieutenant Willoughby in the outbreak of 1857, to prevent its contents falling into the hands of the rebels.

"The old Cemetery of Dehli comes next. Then, passing under the Railway Bridge, the visitor debouches on the

Queen's Road, a spacious roadway running parallel with the line of Railway from the Calcutta Gate of the City to the Moree Gate, both of which have been dismantled. On his immediate right is St. Mary's Catholic Church. Then the Queen's Sarái, a huge structure, with an imposing frontage built by the Municipal Committee, at a cost of Rs. 1,00,570, for the accommodation of Native and European travellers. Next is the entrance to the Queen's Gardens, and further on the East India Railway Terminus. On the left outside angle formed by the level crossing of the Railway line with the Queen's Road, is St. Stephen's Church, belonging to the S. P. G. I. Mission. In advance of this—500 yards—is the Moree Gate. As the visitor debouches from the Railway Bridge (called Lothian Bridge), the lofty walls of the Palace will be seen on his left. If this road is still followed up, it will lead through the Faiz Bazaar to the Dehli Gate, through which the corpses of the sons of the ex-Emperor Bahadur Sháh were brought back after the Princes had been shot dead by Hodson, just subsequent to the complete evacuation of the City by the mutineers in 1857. This part of the town is termed Duriowgunge, where are the lines of a Native Infantry Regiment, and the houses of many European residents.

"The celebrated Chándni Chouk is no longer what it was. Its glories have ceased, and it is unlikely that the scenes of gaudy pomp once there enacted will ever again meet the eye.

"The shops are probably as brave in outward show as they ever were, but the moving throng of richly-dressed nobles riding on caprisoned horses, lounging on their elephants, or borne along in parti-colored palankeens, have passed away for ever.

"The Dehli Institute in the Chándni Chouk will well repay a visit. It is one of the largest buildings in the European style of architecture in this part of India, and is a great ornament to the City. It contains the Station Library, Museum Municipal Office, Darbár-room, and Rooms for social reunions. This structure was erected at the expense of the Municipal Committee at a cost of Rs. 1,35,457.

"Facing the Dehli Institute, on the Chándni Chouk side, is a handsome and well-finished Clock Tower with four faces, and a chime of five bells. The City is indebted for this useful, as well as ornamental, structure also to the Municipal Committee, at a cost of Rs. 25,500. It is 128 feet above the ground.

"The visitor should by no means fail to drive round the

Queen's Gardens, which are very tastefully laid out in the English style. Opposite the Institute, with which the Gardens are connected, is the Band Stand. A branch of Āli Mardán's Canal passes through the Gardens.

"If time can be given, a pleasant drive may be had by leaving the City at the Cashmere Gate, and turning sharp to the left, following up the circular road which goes close to the walls; and passing the Moree, Cábul, Lahore, Fárásh Khánâ, Ājmere, and Tarkomán Gates, entrance to the City can be again made at the Dehli Gate. The road from this last Gate leads to Firoz Sháh's Lát, the Fort of Puráná Killá, Humáyun's Tomb, &c. The road to the Kutab leaves the circular road just about the Lahore Gate."

Outside the Cashmere Gate is the new Cemetery, where lie the mortal remains of John Nicholson, a great soldier, and a man with a great career, apparently, before him: he fell in the attack on Dehli, being mortally wounded in leading the stormers along the inside of the ramparts on the 14th of September, 1857.*

Near the Jamá Masjid, up several intricate lanes, will be found a modern Jain Temple, which contains some handsome carving, and is considered a curiosity by some travellers. This building can be visited between 4 and 5 P.M. In the Chándni Chouk is the Mosque of Roshun-ud-dowláh, from the terrace of which the terrible Nádir witnessed the slaughter of the inhabitants of Dehli in 1732; hard by is the *Kotwáli*, or Chief Police Station, where Hodson exposed the bodies of the Princes whom he slew in 1857. Every spot around seems marked in blood in this home of Imperial Tragedy, happily at peace now.

KALÁN MASJID.

Last in the list of objects for the first day is the *Káli*, more properly *Kalán Masjid*. This, says Harcourt, is only interesting to antiquarians: nevertheless—since there may be some of that class among the visitors to our antiquities—all that is known of this ancient building must here be told.

Situate in the south of the modern town, near the Gate called *Turkmán*, it originally formed part of the City of Firozábád—to be described presently. It was finished, as recorded in an inscription on its walls, A.D. 1386 (*temp.*

* *Vide infra*, p. 61.

Firoz Sháh Toghlak) in the massive unornamented style the second Pathán period.* This severe spirit is quite characteristic of the latter part of the fourteenth century. perhaps, having instructed Masalmán workmen, the architects of the day had dispensed with Hindu aid; perhaps it was merely the material expression of a reaction against Hindu exuberance of all kinds, such as had so strongly infected the earlier architecture of the Patháns in India. A richer style was afterwards to reappear before the introduction of complete electicism under the Moghuls.

The following account of this curious building is borrowed from Cunningham:—

The *Masjid* is a single room 71 feet in length by 41 feet in breadth, with two rows of four pillars, each down the centre and one row of coupled pillars along the front. These column divide the whole area into fifteen squares, each of which i covered by a small dome, the central one being higher than the rest. The walls are thick, and the three openings in them filled with red-stone screen-work. There is a small quadrangular Court in front, and the whole is enclosed by an outer wall of great thickness. On the outside the building consists of two storeys, of which the lower, forming a kind of plinth to the actual place of worship, is 28 feet high, the total height to the top of the battlements being 66 feet. The walls of the upper storey have a number of openings, all of which were once filled with the bold geometrical tracery of the period in white marble. General Cunningham regards this as a characteristic and favourable specimen of the architecture of the fourteenth century. It is supposed to have been originally covered completely with brightly painted plaster, most of which, however, has now disappeared. The rest of the work is still solid and strong; and after the lapse of five centuries is in good preservation.

FIROZABAD.

The tourist who adopts our "Diary" will set out on his second day from the south-east or Dehli-Gate of the modern city, and drive southward, having on his left the old bank of the Jamná, and on his right the old Sanscrit *Prastha*, or "field"

---

* Fergusson's Hist. Archit. II, 655.

(called after the God Indra).* This was one of the five tracts belonging to the five Pándu brothers, which were claimed by their leader as the price of peace. The Kuru Monarch Duryodhan replying that he should have no territory, not so much as could be covered by the point of a needle, the Pandu leader and the other four brothers marched against the King, and overthrew him in the famous field of Kuruchet, not far from the Prastha called Pánipat, where the temporary fate of India has been decided three several times in subsequent days. Cunningham gives reasons for dating these transactions about the middle of the fifteenth century B.C., thus making Dehli contemporaneous with Nineveh and the Exodus. In those days the river flowed about a mile to the westward of its present bed, its course being almost coincident with that of the present road. The first place of interest is the *Kotilá* of Firoz Sháh Toghlak (1351—88) with the stone-pillar. This is a Buddhist remain, brought down from the sub-Himalayan country, where the contemporaries of Antiochus and Ptolemy had one of their chief seats, and has now for ages stood upon the top of a three-storied structure, where it still is. When Finch was here, it had on its top a globe, surmounted with a crescent—the form of pinnacle so common in Indian buildings, and, as was usual, gilt. Hence its name of *Minárá-i-Zurin*, "golden pillar" (*vide* Appendix B). "The golden pillar" is a single shaft of pale pinkish sandstone, 42 feet 7 inches in length, of which the upper portion, 35 feet in length, has received a very high polish, while the remainder is left quite rough. The older inscriptions (for which the pillar was originally erected) comprise the well-known edits of Asoká, which were promulgated in the middle of the third century B.C. in the ancient Páli, or spoken language of the day [a vernacular Sanscrit of Buddhist times, and now the sacred language of some Buddhist countries]. "The inscription ends with a short sentence, in which King Asoká directs the setting up of monoliths in different parts of his Kingdom."—(*Cunningham*.) This pillar is covered with inscriptions dating from the reign of Asoká in the third century before Christ; the names of the contemporaneous Greek sovereigns furnish almost the only certain date in early Indian History (*vide* Appen-

* "Indraprastha," or as corrupted in modern speech, Indraput. The latter name, however, is more specially used, now-a-days, to indicate the city of Humáyun (also called *Dinpanah*) to be found described a little farther on (p. 31).

dix C). A similar pillar was put up at the N. W. part of this same City of Firoz, in his hunting Palace, where Hindu Ráo's house now stands. The inscriptions, as far as they can be traced, are mere duplicates of the first named.

The City of Firoz was upwards of six miles in length by two in average breadth, if it took in the *Khushak Shikár* on the ridge. But Cunningham considers it improbable that the whole of this space was occupied. Its population is estimated by him to have been about 150,000, about that of modern Agra.*

The Palace of Firoz, the remains of which surround the *Kotilá*, formed the nucleus or citadel of this extensive space, but its exact dimensions cannot now be traced. The remarks on the *Kalán Masjid* are illustrative of the style that prevailed in the day when Firozábád was built, and which probably characterised this Palace, the second or middle Pathán school. Its origin is thus described by Fergusson:

"After sustaining a defeat in 1191, Shahab-ud-din (Ghori) entered India in 1193, when he attacked and defeated Pirthee Raj of Dehli. Next year he conquered Canouj, and founded the Pathán empire of India, at the head of which he died in 1206. In this portion of his dominion he was succeeded by Kutub-ud-din Aibuk, a Turkmán, who had risen from slavery to command the army in India. He and his successor Altumsh introduced Pathán architecture; their principal works were in the old Hindu cities at the Kutub. In its first period the style was characterised by all the richness which Hindu elaboration could bestow; in the second, by a stern simplicity and grandeur much more appropriate, according to our ideas, to the spirit of the people; and during the latter part of its existence, by return to the elaborateness of the past, but at this period every detail was fitted to its place and purpose. We forget the Hindu [workman] except in his delicacy, and we recognize one of the completed architectural styles of the world."—*Hist. Archit.*, pp. 645-646.

Before leaving Firozábád, the traveller may be glad to be reminded of an interest of later days attaching to it. Among the ruins of Firoz's Palace it was that the imbecile Emperor Álamgir II. was decoyed to his murder in 1759. The water was then high, and the poor Prince's headless trunk was flung from a window and exposed upon the bank.

* But *vide infra*, p. 66.

Though not in this neighbourhood, the *Kaddam Sharif* or *Fárásh Khánà* may be here mentioned, as showing the extent to which Firozábád stretched in one direction. It is a fortified enclosure of the time of Firoz Sháh, not far from the Lahore Gate of Sháhjahánábád, and has externally much of the not ungrateful strength that marks the stone-mason's work of that era. The inner enclosure is a *Dargáh*, or shrine of stone thickly coated with lime, and containing a low-pillared chamber in which is the tomb of Fatteh Sháh, the King's son, who died in his father's lifetime, A. D. 1374 and who was buried under an impression of the Prophet's foot brought from Mecca by his tutor Makdhum Jaháná. (Such at least is the local tradition.) The chamber, like the cloisters by which it is flanked, is supported upon square pillars with brackets, looking as if they had been taken from a Hindu temple. One of Firoz's masonry tanks is close outside, but is rapidly falling into decay.

INDRAPAT.

Following the old bank the road passes between the *Lál Darwázá* and the *Puráná Killá*, to which the name of *Indrápat* (corruption of Indraprastha) is now especially restricted by the people, and which was once known by the name of *Dinpana*, or "Asylum of the Faith." The *Lál Darwázá*, "this fine and massive gateway" (Cunningham), is a well-preserved specimen of the third period of the style of architecture to which the last remarks refer, and was the Cábul Gate of Sher Sháh's City. The Fort on the opposite side was the citadel and Palace whence Humáyun was expelled by Sher Sháh, and to which he returned to die after his rival's death. The Brentford of these two quarrelsome Kings extended from the *Lál Darwázá* to the south of Humáyun's tomb, and the circuit of the *enceinte* was about double that of Sháhjahánábad or modern Dehli. In January, 1612, Finch entered it from the south, crossing the stream in front of Ájmere Gate by a bridge of eleven arches, known as "the *Bará Pul*," which is still in existence.* The citadel

* William Finch, the merchant mariner, whose visit to Dehli has been above referred to, and whose journal is abstracted in *Purchas, Lib. iv. Ch.* 4, did not, of course, see Dehli as we know it. His "Dely" was the city of Sher Sháh and Humáyun, and, with the exception of the last named monarch's Mausoleum (which he saw filled with his relics) was in almost as desolate a state as now. He

of Humáyun (called Shergarh and Sháhgarh during his exile) is but small. He appears to have begun the structure, as it now stands, in 1533 A.D., but his rival, on his expulsion, strengthened and beautified it seven years later, the circuit of the walls is little more than a mile; in shape it is almost rectangular. The interior is now filled up with native huts, *pauperum tabernæ*; but royal towers are not wanting; and the *Killá Koná* Mosque is the finest known specimen of the third Pathán period, about 1540, just before this school of art was about to merge in the more ambitious electric style of the earlier Moghuls. The front is at once massive and elegant; consisting of a crenellated sky-line, with small pinnacles at the corners, and a fine bold dome, of true structural outline, in the centre. This Mosque is wonderfully sharply carved, as well in the red-stone as in the marble; and the effect is both broad and refined. It is entered by five arches, exhibiting a slight tendency to the horse-shoe form, and thrown back from high and deeply-embayed portals, of a similar shape, though larger size. All are ornamented with slate, marble, and coloured stone; and the interior still preserves considerable traces of enamelling. Fergusson (*Hist. Archit.*, 655) thus describes the class to which this Mosque belongs:—

"The facades of these Mosques became far more ornamental and more frequently encrusted with marbles, and always adorned with sculpture of a rich and beautiful character; the angles of the buildings were often ornamented with little kiosques, supported by four richly bracketed pillars, but never with minarets. . . . , The call to prayer was made from the roof . . . The Patháns seem to have regarded the Minár as the Italians viewed the Campanile, more as a symbol of power and of victory than as an adjunct to a house of worship."

Hard by is the *Sher Mandir* or *Mundal*, an octagonal building of three stories, said to have been used as a library, and bearing traces, of having been once decorated within with mural painting. It was from the top of this that the restored Humáyun fell, having risen too suddenly after the

tells us, I know not on what authority, that it was the Rheims of the Moghuls; "The Kings of India must here be crowned, or else they are held usurpers." He adds that "it is seated in a goodly plain, environed with goodly pleasant gardens and monuments." In those days the neighbourhood was "all inhabited by Googers."

In the copy of Purchas that I have consulted, Finch does not speak of "seven castles," but of nine. So also de Laet (*vide* the abstract translation by Prof. Lethbridge).

call to prayer from the adjacent Mosque. He appears to have fallen down one flight of the staircase, and to have lain at the foot for some time stunned: on recovering his senses he walked home, but the injuries were more serious than at first supposed, and proved fatal after a short illness, 26th January, 1556.—*Journ. As. Soc., XL*, 133.

HUMAYUN'S TOMB.

This Emperor's Mausoleum is a mile or so south of the Fort. It was commenced by the deceased monarch's widow Háji Begam; and completed by his son and successor Akbar, who is said to have spent fifteen lakhs of rupees on it and sixteen years of labour. It is interesting as forming the first known example of the style of sepulchre afterwards to become so famous in the Taj of Agra, another conjugal monument nearly a century later in date. It is the earliest work of the Moghul period; and presents some of the peculiarities by which that school is distinguished. Cunningham thus describes the building:—"The exterior form . . . is a square with the corners cut off on an octagon with four long and four short faces, and each of the short faces forms one side of the four octagonal corner towers. In this tomb we first see towers attached to the four angles of the main building . . . they form an important innovation in the Mahammadan architecture of Northern India, which was gradually improved and developed, until it culminated in the graceful Minárs of the Taj Mahal . . . Another innovation observable in this tomb is the narrow-necked dome which was afterwards adopted in all the Moghul buildings."

It must not be supposed from these concluding words that the dome of the Tomb is of the bulbous shape of those at the Táj or at Sháhjahán's Mosque in Dehli. On the contrary, the termination of the hemisphere is marked by a firmly-moulded cornice, which gives this dome a bold and graceful curve that it would have been well had its successors understood and maintained. This dome has been estimated to be three-fourths the size of that of St. Paul's, London. Nevertheless in its large marble dome and side kiosques, its majestic portals, and storeyed openings, its lofty plinth with doorways, this building is clearly the forerunner of the Táj. Instead, however, of the unmixed and unsullied material which renders the later edifice so unique, the basement of this tomb largely employs stone, though white marble forms the facing of the domes and the decoration of the lower structure. The side chambers contain the tombs of many of the house of Timur, and on the platform is that of the luckless Dára Shekoh, eldest son of Sháhjahán, slain by the bigoted usurper Aurungzeb (his younger brother) in 1659. The central hall is famous in modern times as the temporary retreat of the Royal Family, and in September, 1857, for the bold conduct of Major Hodson and Lieutenant Macdowell, who, attended only by a few native troopers, entered the enclosure and took out the sons of the ex-King Bahádur Sháh, whom Hodson executed with his own hand the same day.

The following remarks are by a well-informed writer in *Indian Public Opinion*:—

"When Humáyun died, Akbar, a child of thirteen, was at Lahore; the funeral must have been conducted under the direction of Háji Begum, whose relation to her husband was that of a companion, as well as of an adviser. The Mausoleum was commenced by Háji Begum, but it was finished by Akbar at a cost of fifteen lacs of rupees, and is said to have occupied two hundred masons daily for sixteen years. The ashes of Humáyun repose with those of five of his descendants who wore the crown of Dehli, and of eleven others who were the councillors, generals, and friends of Kings. Out of the eighteen marble tombs erected in this magnificent building, only one gives the name of the honoured dead; it was with considerable difficulty that we succeeded in identifying the grave of the unfortunate Dára, a Prince in whose history there is much that puts us in mind of the military ardour of Rupert and the ill-fated popularity of Monmouth."

Opposite Humáyun's tomb will be found some works of the later Pathán and first Moghul styles. The earlier and larger is the Mosque of Esá Khán, about 1545 A.D, and it is worth a visit. Fifteen or sixteen years later was built the neighbouring tomb of Akbar's foster-father, murdered by Adham Khán (*vide infra*, p. 53); and the traveller can see, by comparing these two, what was the nature of the transition that took place at this epoch.

Several small and very beautiful cemeteries remain to be visited before leaving this neighbourhood.

NIZAMUDIN.

The enclosure to this cemetery is entered by an unimportant gateway. The first building, the *Chaursat Kambá* (or "sixty-four pillars"), contains the tomb of Aziza Kokal Tásh, the foster-brother of the great Akbar, and several others of less interest. It is a marble hall with twenty-five small domes, and the pillars that support them from within form elegant groined arches. On all four sides is a carved screen of white marble. The building is a curious one, and a good specimen of the period of Akbar (the 1st Moghul). It seems to have been intended for a canopy to a family vault.

Further on is an enclosure formed round the tomb of the great Aulia adventurer Sháh Nizámudin, who served under the Emperor Alá-ud-din Khilji about the end of the thirteenth century. He is said by some to have been a sorcerer, by others, an assassin of the Secret Society of Khorásán. Sleeman was of opinion that he was the founder of Thuggism, as the Thugs profess a special reverence for his memory.*

There is considerable ground for suspecting him of complicity in the death of the Emperor Toghlak Sháh, 1325. He is said to have promised the son Empire, and to have foretold that the Emperor would never come to Dehli. And, when he heard of his nearing the Palace, he only remarked, "*Hinoz Dilli dur ast*" (Dehli is still far). The heir-apparent received his father in a magnificent pavilion at Áfghánpur, which had been erected for the occasion. Immediately on the Emperor's entrance he was crushed by the fall of the roof. The son who thus succeeded became the notorious tyrant Mahammad Ibn Toghlak.† It appears, however, from Ibn Batuta's narrative that Nizámudin was dead when these events occurred, although he is accused of having instigated the parricide at an earlier period. The saying about the distance from Dehli is there attributed to "the astrologers." It has since become proverbial, like the Scotch saying, "Its a far cry to Loch Awe."

The tomb has a very graceful appearance, and is surrounded by a verandah of white marble, while a pierced marble screen encloses the sarcophagus, which is always covered with a cloth. Round the grave-stone runs a carved wooden guard, and from the four corners rise stone pillars draped with cloth, which support an angular wooden frame-work, and which has some-

* This man's history would probably reward careful inquiry.

† *Vide* Appendix D.

thing of the appearance of a canopy to a bed. Below this wooden canopy there is stretched a cloth of a green and red, much the worse for wear. The interior of the tomb is covered with painted characters in Arabic, and at the head of the grave is a stand with a Korán. The marble screen is very richly cut, and the roof of the arcade-like verandah is finely painted in a flower pattern.

The Moghul dome is of the era of Akbar, and further additions and improvements have been made since, which somewhat impair the harmony of the work by blending different and somewhat remote styles.

Flanking this Mausoleum is the celebrated *Jamát Khánú* Mosque, a fine specimen of the gloomy style that preceded the architecture of Firoz, and called here "the 2nd Pathán." On the face is an inscription on a small plaque in the wall; the last line of which contains a chronogram yielding the date 725H. (= 1326, *vide Agra Handbook, Appendix.*)

Contemporary with this hero was the Poet Khusru, who now lies buried near him. "He moved about where he pleased through the Palace of the Emperor Toghlak Sháh 500 years ago, and sang *extempore* to his lyre, while the greatest and the fairest watched his lips to catch the expressions as they came warm from his soul. His popular songs are still the most popular, and he is one of the favored few who live through ages in the every-day thoughts and feelings of many millions, while the crowned heads that patronised him in their brief day of pomp and power are forgotten or remembered merely as they happen to be connected with him."—*General Sleeman's Rambles.*

It is interesting to find that, though he was a man of no special sanctity, the squalid posterity of the neighbourhood still tend the Poet's greatest The lines on the headstone outside the mortuary chamber contain his nickname of "The Parrot," and the concluding double chronogram yields 725 H., the same date as that of the *Jamát Khánú* Mosque.

In the same enclosure is the modern tomb of Mirza Jahángir. The tomb itself, raised some few feet from the ground, is entered by steps, and is enclosed in a beautiful carved marble screen, the sarcophagus being covered with a very artistic representation of leaves and flowers chiselled in marble. Mirza Jahángir was the son of Akbar II., and the tomb was built in A.D. 1832. The tomb of Jahánárá Begum is also in the same cemetery with the above; the sarcophagus is enclosed in a marble screen. Jahánárá Begum was the daughter of the Emperor Sháhjahán, and sister to the unfortunate Dára Shekho, the heir-apparent to Sháhjabán's throne, easily defeated and put to death by his younger brother, Aurungzeb, who deposed his father, and mounted the throne in his place. Jahánárá was a famous beauty of whom the European travellers of those days have many sad tales to tell. She refused to share the guilty glory of Aurungzeb's Court, and preferred to stay with her father in his captivity at Agra. Aurungzeb is suspected of having removed her to Dehli to murder her. Tavernier saw her removal from Agra (as he understood) by order of Aurungzeb. She was brought to Dehli by the tyrant, and she lived there for many years, surviving her sister, and not dying till A.D. 1681. On her tomb are these words,—a part of the inscription is said to have been written by herself:—"Let no rich coverlet adorn my grave: this grass is the best covering for the tomb of the poor in spirit, the humble, the transitory Jahánárá, the disciple of the holy men of Chist, the daughter of the Emperor Sháhjahán." It was for this Moghul Cordelia that Sháhjahán built the Jamá Masjid of Agra. "The holy men of Chist" are the Fakirs of Ájmere. One of whom in the preceding century had been Shekh Salim, the founder of Fathpur-Sikri.

Still in the same enclosure is the tomb of the incompetent Mahammad Sháh, Emperor from 1719 to 1748, whose last days on the Peacock Throne have been already glanced at in describing the Palace of Sháhjahánábád. It was in this long and inglorious reign that the massacre of the citizens took place by order of Nádir Sháh.

Hard by is Nizámudin's Bauli, or well-house, similar to so many here and at Agra, and described in the first of this series. A cheap sensation is to be had by giving certain boys a few coppers to reward them for jumping into the water feet foremost.

This special interest of this small cemetery is its containing specimens of carved and pierced marble work of five centuries ready for comparison.

THE ROAD TO THE KUTAB.

The tourist who pursues the instructions contained in the commencement of this *Guide* will return to Dehli (Sháhjahánábád) from his visit to the places last described, and set out again the next morning for the *Kutab Minár*, a drive of about 11 miles, which is the Appian way of Dehli (as the Sikandra road is of Agra), and has on either hand more tombs than could be either visited or described to any useful purpose. We will suppose him to take this road in the early dawn, in order to save time for sight-seeing. He will perhaps at first—if in winter—have a somewhat cold drive, in the course of which he will pass on one hand the *Jantar Mantur*, on the other the Mausoleum of Sufdár Jang. In the former, he will see a "folly" of the last century, in the shape of an observatory constructed for the Emperor Mahammad Shah, about 1730 A.D. by Jai Singh, Rájáh of Jaipur, of which the following is a good description, taken from Beresford's *Delhi*:—"The largest of the buildings is an immense equatorial dial named by the Rájáh the Semrat Yantar, or Prince of Dials: the dimensions of the gnomon being as follows:—

Length of hypothenuse	118·5	feet.
" " base ...	104·0	"
" " perpendicular	56·75	"

"This is now much injured. At a short distance, nearly in front of the great dial, is another building in somewhat better preservation; it is also a sun-dial, or rather several dials combined in one building. In the centre is a staircase leading to the top, and its side walls form gnomons to concentric semicircles, having a certain inclination to the horizon, and they represent meridians removed by a certain angle from the meridian of the Observatory. The outer walls form gnomons to graduated quadrants, one to the east and the other to the west. A wall connects the four gnomons, and on its northern face is described a large quadrilateral semicircle for taking the altitudes of the celestial bodies. Lying east and west to the south of the great equatorial dial stand two circular buildings open at the top, and each having a pillar in the centre: from the bottom of the pillar thirty horizontal radii of stone, gradually increasing in breadth till they recede from it, are built to the circular wall: each of these forms a sector of six degrees, and the corresponding spaces between the radii being of the same dimensions, make up the circle of 360 degrees. In the wall at the spaces between the radii and recesses, on either side of which are square holes at convenient distances, to enable the observer to climb to such heights as was necessary to read off the observation, each of the recesses had two windows, or rather openings, many of which have been since built up. On the edge of the recesses are marked the tangents of the degrees of the sun's altitude, as shown by the shadow of the pillar, and numbered from 1 to 45 degrees. When the sun exceeds that height, the degrees are marked on the radii, numbered from the pillar in such a manner as to show the complement of its altitude; these degrees are subdivided into minutes, but the opposite spaces in the walls have no sub-division, being merely divided into six parts of one degree each; the shadow of the sun falling on either of the divisions show the sun's azimuth; in like manner lunar and stellar altitudes and azimuths may be observed. These two buildings, being exactly alike in all respects, were doubtless designed to correct errors by comparing the results of different observations obtained at the same instant of time."—*Beresford's Delhi*, 1856.

The monument of Safdar Jang is also a monument of the degradation which befel Moghul architecture in the century that followed the building of the Táj at Agra. On this subject the following remarks of Mr. Fergusson should be collated:—

"With Aurangzeb the decline [of art] set in steadily and rapidly, and before his death the art of the Moghuls had perished. When that monarch* was residing at Aurangábád between the years 1650—1657, he lost his favourite daughter, and in honour of her memory ordered his architects to produce an exact copy of his father's celebrated tomb, the Táj Mahal. They believed they were doing so, but the difference between the two monuments is startling."—*Hist. Archit., II.*, 687.

The difference indeed must have been rather one of place than of time, for the Táj itself was not finished till 1648, nor the Moti Masjid of Agra till six years later. Still even those buildings show the commencement of decadence in some of their lines; and when Safdár Jang died a hundred years later, the decay of taste was accomplished. This pretentious but somewhat unsuccessful effort is thus described in the Guide-book of Captain Harcourt:

"The Mausoleum is situated in a garden enclosed on the four sides by a wall, at the corners of which are pavilions of red sandstone. On three sides of the garden, which may be over 300 yards square, there are apartments for visitors."

The Mausoleum stands on a terrace; beneath this, says Beresford in his book on Dehli (1856), "is a vault containing a grave of plain earth, covered with a cloth strewed daily with fresh flowers. In the centre of the first floor is a beautiful marble sarcophagus, elegantly carved and highly polished. The building is surmounted by a marble dome"

* He was not a Monarch then, but Viceroy of the Deccan.—H. G. K.

(this is now very much out of repair), and as a Mausoleum is a "remarkable and majestic structure. It was erected by Nawáb Shujá-u-douláh, son of Safdár Jang." Some of the details are graceful, especially the doming and ceiling of the various chambers. But the material employed on the decoration is plaster; and the building generally shows an absence of industrious handiwork which makes it an unfavourable contrast with the conscientious specimens of labour in the neighbourhood.

Safdár Jang did not, perhaps, deserve a better monument. His lot was cast in villainously selfish times; and the best that can be said for him is that others were as bad as he. The nephew of the wily immigrant Saádat Khán—a Shiáh adventurer from Khorásán, who became Viceroy of Oudh, and Vazir of the Empire—Safdár Jang succeeded his uncle, sometimes in one capacity, sometimes in another. Overthrown in Dehli politics by the bold and crafty Gháziuddin (grandson of the old Turkmán noble, who founded the dynasty of Hyderábád), Safdár Jang held aloof while the feeble Emperor Ahmad Sháh rushed upon his fate. Before his disgrace he had occupied himself with endeavouring to introduce something like administration into the distracted province of Rohilkhand, from which he had expelled the former conqueror, a Pathán or Afghán, named Ali Mohamad. And now while the Court and Cabinet were torn by murderous intrigues, Safdár Jang once more turned his attention to these neighbours of his, and tried, for purposes of his own, to sow strife amongst them. He died in 1754 before his machinations had taken any very active form; but he bequeathed his policy to his son, in whose hands it bore well-known fruits—to him and to his English allies.* It should be added that *Safdár Jang* was only a title signifying "Piercer of Battle ranks," the real name of the statesman being Mansur Áli Khán. And his tomb has interest, both on account of the part played by its occupant in the politics of the Moghul Empire in its decadence, and in virtue of its being the last grand effort of Moghul architecture. From Safdár Jang's tomb there is a cross road to that of Humáyun, a distance of three miles, on the left of which in the township of Khairpúr and nearly opposite the gate of the first named Mausoleum, is a group of four tombs, and a Mosque, probably of the third Pathán period, which General Cunningham thus describes:—

"The northern group," says General Cunningham in a

* *Vide Keene's Moghul Empire.*

letter to the Secretary of the Local Fund Committee of Dehli, "consisting of two *octagonal* tombs and a bridge of seven arches, is attributed by the natives to the time of the Lodi family; the larger tomb, within a square, being assigned to Sekander Lodi, and I believe that this attribution is most probably correct. But the southern group, which consists of a Masjid and two square tombs, belongs, in my opinion, to an earlier period. I am led to this conclusion by the style of the building, which is quite distinct from that of the Lodi period" (A.D. 1450 to A.D. 1526) as well "as from that of the Sáyad dynasty" (A.D. 1414 to A.D. 1444). "If we may judge by the solitary specimen of Sáyad Mobárik's Tomb on the other hand, the style of the Masjid agrees precisely with that of Feroz's great Mosque in Ferozábád (no longer existing) as described by Timour's historians, as well as with that of another Masjid of Feroz which formerly existed at Depálpore, in the Panjab."

General Cunningham, in his official report of the state of the buildings about Dehli, considers that "the Masjid attached to these buildings is the only existing specimen of the ornamented Mosque of the time of Feroz, which so much attracted the attention of Timour" (or Tamerlane, in A.D. 1398, when he ravaged India,) "that he carried off all the masons who had built it to Samárkand, that they might erect another like it in his capital. The Mosque of Ferozábád is described by Ferishtá as covered with inscriptions detailing the ordinances issued by Feroz. Of this Mosque only the back wall is now standing, but the Masjid, as above mentioned, which I wish to see cleared, corresponds exactly with the description of the historian. Its front is entirely covered with inscriptions and draperied ornaments in a very hard plaster, which is still fresh and sharp, after the lapse of five centuries. The interior walls are also thickly covered with inscriptions and ornaments cut in hard stone, which are now as perfect as when first executed." This beautiful building will reward the short walk required to reach it. The tomb on the south side of the courtyard is also very handsome and well-preserved; and its dome is as finely shaped and proportioned as any in Europe. These works appear to belong to a somewhat later and more ornate style than that assigned to them by Cunningham, and I do not think they can be much earlier than the tomb supposed to be that of Sikandar Lodi (1500 A.D.)

In the neighbourhood will be found the Hauz Khás and tomb of Firoz Sháh (*Circ.* A.D. 1388), and buildings of the same period (the second or undecorated Pathán) at Begampur and Roshan Chirágh.

BEGAMPUR, ETC.

Begampur is a curious old specimen of Pathán workmanship, a good deal larger than Kirkhi, to which it still presents so many features of general resemblance, that there is very little hesitation in putting the date of erection some time in Firoz Sháh's reign. Mr. Stephen dates it 1387. This is a massive enclosure approached by a flight of stairs, which are in a very dilapidated state. It lies about 800 yards to the left of the road leading from Dehli to the Kutab, and is some three miles from the latter.

The place was possibly a Palace, and it is marked by the square pillars, lancet-arches, and general air of puritan and unadorned sternness, which mark the second Pathán period of architecture. On the west side is a disused Mosque, with a very grand embayed portal and a vault of massive simplicity.

"The walled town of Roshan Chirágh Dehli is about two miles to the E. Roshan Chirágh is a shrine erected to the memory of Sheikh Násir-ud-din Mohamad, and was built by Firoz Sháh, who reigned from A.D. 1351 to A.D. 1385. The tomb of Sultán Behlol Lodi, who reigned from A.D. 1450 to A.D. 1488, lies behind that of the saint. The interior of the court is filled with various tombs, more or less worthy of inspection, and kept in fair order. The town itself is a poor place, with nothing in it to recommend it to the notice of the visitor: it used to have three gateways, but two of these being considered unsafe were closed."—*Harcourt.*

BUDDI MANZIL, OR BURJ MANDAL.

Opposite the Begampur enclosure is a strange heap of ruins called *Buddi Manzil*, possibly the remains of a hunting-lodge. Nothing now remains of it but a domed pavilion, flanked by a four-sided turret or bastion, from the top of which there is a good view. It can hardly have been within any of the cities of the neighbourhood, and was probably a mere "folly" of one of the Pathán Princes of the "second period."

THE VILLAGE OF HAUZ KHAS

Lies some four or five miles to the north of the Kutab, and is approached most easily from Safdár Jang's tomb. There is no carriage road to it. It contains what is called Firoz Sháh's bath or tank, and a tomb said to have been built by Mahomed Sháh (A.H. 762).

Timur says in his memoirs:—

"This is a reservoir which was constructed by Sultán Firoz Sháh, and faced all round with stone and cement. Each side is more than a bow-shot long, and there are buildings round it. The tank is filled by the rain during the rainy season; it supplies the neighbourhood with water during the year. The tomb of Firoz Sháh stands upon the bank." The area of the tank is over a hundred bigáhs, but is now a complete ruin, the surface being used for cultivation. Firoz Sháh, who died in A.D. 1388, is buried in a tomb close by.

KIRKHI.

Not far from Begampur, and some three miles to the right of the road turning to Dehli, and two and-a-half from the Kutab, will be found a Fort and Mosque of the same period in the village of *Kirkhi*, of which the following is a description:—

"The Mosque of Kirkhi is an enormous structure situated on high ground, and is built of dark-colored granite, and cased all over with black chunam, which gives it a very sombre appearance. It is a square, supported at the four corners by towers nearly 50 feet high; has two storeys, and is crowned with 89 small domes of very plain but most solid construction. The whole building is in excellent preservation, with the exception of the north-east angle, the roof of which has fallen in, not however from decay, but from the effects of a fire said to have occurred some 70 years ago. The basement storey consists of 104 small cells with arched ceilings, each cell being about 9 feet square. There is also a cell beneath each door, and one in each turret, making in all 112 cells. There are three doors leading to the upper storey, *viz.*, to the south-east and north; the latter is alone open now. As you enter in front and to the right and left, there are triple cloisters, supported on single, double, and quadruple pillars."—*From the Records of the Dehli Archælogical Society*, 1850.

These buildings should by all means be inspected, being architecturally most important, if not beautiful.

Lastly may be mentioned certain works of the last Pathán period.

THREE TOMBS CALLED THE TIR BURJA.

These stand to the left of the road from Safdár Jang's Tomb to the Kuarb, close to the village of Mobárikpore, and are somewhat difficult of access for the equestrian. The names they bear are respectively Barrá Khán, Chotá Khán, and Káli Khán. The largest, Barrá Khán, is perhaps of the earlier Pathán period, but the date of erection is unknown. They are all, more or less, in a state of decay, like hundreds of others which lie around neglected, and are built of red sandstone and kharra-stone. They are hardly worthy of a visit, and a general idea of them may be obtained from the road.

MOBARIKPUR KOTLA.

The tomb of Mobárik Sháh is in the village of Mobárik-pore, close to the three tombs just alluded to. The date of erection is somewhere between A.D. 1540 and A.D. 1545, during the reign of Sher Sháh. The building is in the Pathán style of architecture of kharra-stone.—*Harcourt.*

THE OLD HINDU FORTS.

Arrived at the Kutab, the visitor finds himself on the scene of one of India's older authentic periods. Here, according to the best authorities, was an extensive city of the *Sákás*, a tribe overthrown by Vikramádit II. about A. D. 78. After this period it ceased to be a royal residence, though the iron pillar is determined by Cunningham to have been set up here by one of the *Guptá* Rájáhs in A.D. 319. Subsequent to which there appear to be no authentic notices of this—the original Dehli or Dilli—till it was rebuilt in the middle of the eighth century by Anang Pál, the first King of the Tamárs, a Rájput tribe. It is supposed by Cunningham that Dehli soon after once more ceased to be a royal city, and fell into decay, to be again rebuilt by a Rájá of the same dynasty and the same name, Anang Pál II., who was driven hither from Kanoj, his ancestral metropolis. However this be, certain it is that this Tamár dynasty ruled, at one time or other, over a considerable extent of territory between the Himálayá and the Vindhyan range; that their capital was in this neighbourhood, its citadel being the enclosure which now surrounds the Kutab Minár; and that they were overthrown, about the middle of the twelfth century, by another Rájput tribe, the Chauháns. These latter added to the fortifications, and after a reign of about forty years, were in turn overthrown by the Masalmáns under Shahábudin Ghorí, and his general, Kutab-ud-din, in 1193.

It was the last of this brief dynasty, Prithwi Ráj, or Rái Pithorá, who added to the Lállkot—the "Red Fort" round the sites of the Kutab Minár—the outwork to the N. E. which still bears his name. "From the north-western angle of the Lállkot," says Cunningham, "the lines of Rái Pithorá's walls can be distinctly traced, running towards the north for about half a mile. From this point they turn to the south of east for one and-a-half miles, then to the south for one mile, and lastly to the west and north-west for three-quarters of a mile, where they join the Lállkot, which being situated on higher ground forms a lofty citadel that completely commands the Fort of Rái Pithorá."

The area of the two together is rather more than half that of the modern city of Sháhjahánábád. General Cunningham elsewhere furnishes the following additional particulars:

The Fort of Lállkot, built in A. D. 1060, is 2¼ miles round. Its walls are lofty and massive; the ramparts averaging near 30 feet in thickness, the parapets being just one-half, or 14¾ feet. These walls have a general height of 60 feet above the bottom of the ditch, and to the extent of about half their original quantity are still in good preservation; having enormous bastions at all the salient angles. The long lines of curtains are relieved by numerous smaller towers well splayed out at the base, and still standing out to a height of 30 feet. In the western portion—which is the best preserved—the gateways, three in number, can be still made out; they appear to have been 17 feet wide, and to have been protected by portcullises.

The Fort of Rái Pithorá appears to have been built after the incursions of the Masalmáns had begun, as an additional protection to the city from the quarter whence such attacks were the most to be apprehended. Its circuit is nearly 4½ miles larger, but far less defensible than the older fort. It is believed to have had ten gates in all, of which at least eight are still traceable. It possessed 27 Hindu or Buddhist temples, hundreds of whose pillars have been worked into the Mosque of the conquerors, and are still standing.

General Cunningham holds that the iron shaft that stands in the quadrangle of the Mosque north-west of the Kutab Minár is the oldest relic of the vanished Hindu city. It is to be presumed, he says, that the pillar must have been erected in some conspicuous position, either within the old city, or close to it. He is not unwilling to allow a similar antiquity to one or two of the stone columns now worked into the body of the great Mosque in which the pillar stands; but with these exceptions he concludes that nothing now exists here that is older than the tenth or eleventh century.

The total height of the pillar above ground is 22 feet, but its depth underground (formerly believed to be much greater) was ascertained, by one of General Cunningham's assistants, in 1872, to be only about 3 feet. Excavations showed that the pillar ended in a knob resting on eight strong bars secured to stone-blocks, somewhat in emulation of Nature's engineering as seen in the roots of a tree. It is believed to be of malleable iron, not cast, but built up by the welding together (by heat and hammering) of successive horizontal cylinders of metal. It slopes a little towards the top, where it is surmounted by a capital over three feet high formed of a series of bevelled rims one above the other. Its meagre history is found recorded in an inscription of six Sanscrit lines cut upon its western face, from which we find that it is claimed as the memorial of Rájáh Dhává, or Bhává, considered by Prinsep to have reigned in the third or fourth century of the Christian era. An old prophecy, already current in the days of the Ghaznevide invader, alleged that the Hindu Government should endure as long as the pillar stood. The remaining inscriptions on the Iron Pillar are unimportant; as are also the babbling traditions collected by travellers about its foot piercing the head of the world-serpent. When human fancies throw a light on opinions that have affected the destinies of nations or the revolutions of empires it becomes interesting to examine them; but the nonsense of the ethnical nursery is of no more value than Little Bopeep or Old Daddy Longlegs. Harcourt attempts indeed to connect the tradition with the final fall of the Hindu power, but it is probably more ancient.

The only other Hindu relics appear in the numerous pillars

of the cloisters above referred to, which belonged to the 27 temples taken down to construct the Mosque of the Moslem conquerors.

On the subject of this Mosque, Fergusson (*Hist. Archit. II.*, 646) thus remarks:—

"To understand these ruins it is necessary to bear in mind that all the pillars are Hindu, and all the walls of Mahomedan architecture . . . indeed it seems probable that the whole structure was re-arranged in the form we now see by the Masalmáns . . . It is so purely Jain that it should perhaps have been noticed in speaking of that style; but as forming a part of the earliest Mosque in India it is now appropriately introduced in this place" [as will be seen more clearly from Cunningham the structure as now seen is Masalmán compiled out of Hindu or Jain, details]. "The pillars are of the same order as those used on Mount Ábu, but much richer and more elaborate . . . In some instances the figures that were on the shafts of the pillars have been cut off, as offensive to Mahomedan strictness . . . but on the less seen parts . . . may still be detected."

The west side is formed by enormous arches (or rather sham arches), the largest of which is said by Fergusson to be 22 feet wide and 53 feet high. Behind this range, at the distance of 32 feet, are the foundations of another wall. "It seems probable that the Hindu pillars between were the only portion proposed to be roofed; some of them are built into the back part of the great arches, and all above is quite plain and smooth without the least trace of any intention to construct a roof or vault of any sort." He goes on to show that the employment of Hindu artizans ignorant of the constructive principles of the arch led to the pointed openings being made on the same principles as those used in Hindu domes. "They carried them up in horizontal courses as far as they could; and then closed them by long slabs meeting at the top." In ornamenting the face of this range they repeated the ornaments of the interior pillars.

The Mosque, of which plans on a scale of 100 feet to one inch are given both in Fergusson and in Cunningham, must, when finally completed, have been one of the grandest in the world. The face of the arcade, of which the arches now remaining are those that have been restored by the British Government, was richly decorated; though the fact of the arches being only arched in appearance, and really no more than struts or brackets, betrays the employment of Hindu artizans unacquainted with the constructive principle of the arch. Within, a sort of pillared hall, 135 feet long, is, by Cunningham, as well as by Fergusson, believed to have been the original Mosque covered by a roof supported by five rows of pillars. Over the opposite entrance is the date A. H. 589, or A. D. 1193; and here, as elsewhere, occurs the name of the conqueror Kutab-ud-din, the victorious Lieutenant of Mahamad Ghori, who overthrew the kingdom of Rái Pithorá in that year. Nothing can surpass the endless variety of the sculptures on the pillars inside and out of this Mosque, except it be their sharpness and delicacy. They were originally plastered over by their bigoted adapters, a circumstance to which perhaps they are indebted for some part of their preservation.

It has been determined by Cunningham that the quadrangle of which these pillars form the cloisters was intended by the Masalmán conquerors as an entrance-court to the Mosque from the eastward.

During the reign of Altamsh (A.D. 1211—36), vast additions were made to this Court; and the Kutab Minár was included in the south-east side of the enclosure, the whole front of the new and old structures combined being now 384 feet, with a breadth of 220 feet. The entire number of Hindu pillars brought into use in these works, from first to last, is estimated at not less than six hundred.

A still further addition was made by Álá-ud-din Khiljí (in A.D. 1300), in the form of an eastern annex, the same breadth as before, and about one-half the original depth.

THE KUTAB.

This magnificent tower, the glory of Dehli, as the Táj is of Agra, is just over 238 feet high, sloping from the foot, from a diameter 47-3 feet to one of scarcely 9. The shaft is divided into five storeys, of which the first and last make up one-half, the second, third, and fourth the other half, of the total height. The basement storey has 24 faces in the form of convex flutings alternately semi-circular and rectangular; in the second storey the projections are all circular; in the third all angular; the fourth is a plain cylinder, and the fifth storey is partly fluted and partly plain. So accurate are the proportions of the three lower storeys that the lines, except when intercepted, run up in one and the same straight line. The intercepting lines are those of balconies going the whole round of the tower, and girdling it with belts of rich projecting pendentives in the purest style of the first Pathán period. The three lower storeys are also belted with bands of ornamental scroll-work containing Arabic inscriptions containing verses from the Korán and the name and praises of the conqueror by whose General the building was commenced. These three lower storeys are all of red stone, probably the original erection of Kutab-ud-din Aibak and his successor Altamsh; the fourth and, to some extent, the fifth storeys are of white marble, showing the restorations of Firoz Sháh Toghlak, about 150 years after the original building was completed.

"The lower storey is 94 feet 11 inches in height, and the upper storey is 22 feet 4 inches, the two measurements together being just equal to half the height of the column: the length of the second storey is 50 feet 8½ inches, the third is 40 feet 9½ inches, the fourth is 25 feet 4 inches, or just one-half of the height of the second storey. Omitting, then, only the stump of the old cupola, the column is just five diameters in height, and the lower storey is just two diameters in height. The circumference of the base is equal to the sum of the diameter of the six storeys of the building, the old cupola being considered as a sixth storey."—*General Cunningham.* In 1794 the pillar was over 242 feet high, but as the capital was injured, Fergusson considers that probably 20 feet might be added to make up the proper height. The minaret of the Mosque of Hassan at Cairo is known to be loftier than this pillar, "but as the Minár is an independent building, it has a far nobler appearance, and both in design and finish far surpasses its Egyptian rival, as indeed it does any building of its class."—*Fergusson.*

The name of this tower originates in a contraction of *Kutab-ud-din ká Minár.* The founder Kutab-ud-din Aibak was the Lieutenant of the Ghorian conqueror of India, who long ruled here as Viceroy, and eventually as King or Emperor. At his death, after a brief period of disturbance, his favourite slave succeeded by the title of Shams-ud-din Altamsh, and the tower was completed in his reign, to serve as a *Maziná* or Muezzin's station for the Mosque *Kutab-ul-Islám.* [*Kutab*, or *Qutb*, according to scientific transliteration, means the "Polar Star."] Fergusson, after giving the measurements, and justly extolling this noble tower, notes the influence of Hindu practice in some features of the workmanship, and makes the valuable suggestion that they were suggested by the Jain buildings of the old city that were doubtless standing in abundance all round when the work was commenced. The occurrence of the names of Aibak and his suzerain Bin Sám on the basement storey is justly regarded by General Cunningham as ground for concluding that the building was begun by the one during the lifetime of the other, which fixes the date of the foundation about the end of the twelfth century. The inscription on the second storey, coupled with the description of Abulfeda in A.D. 1300, shews that the original work was completed by Altamsh, about twenty years after its commencement by his master and predecessor. As already indicated, the completion of the tower, as now seen, is due to the much-building Emperor Firoz Sháh about the third quarter of the fourteenth century.*

Before leaving the Kutab, a word must be said for the finial designed for the tower in 1826 by Major Smith. It is certainly not in harmony with the rest of the building, but neither do the parts of the building harmonize with each other; the stern unadorned cylinders of Sultán Firoz being out of keeping with the barbaric richness of the sloping storeys of red stone on which they stand. The tower sadly requires some termination, its present flat top is suggestive of nothing so much as a factory chimney. Even poor Smith's design would be an improvement; but it ought not to be difficult to put up a dome on four arches of true Pathán taste that would form an appropriate crown to the work. Moreover, a visitor, ascending to the summit, ought to have some shade and shelter when he gets there.

OTHER BUILDINGS.

Besides the eastern annex, mentioned already, Alá-ud-din (1295—1316) added to the Kutab Mosque the splendid southern gateway that still bears his name, and which Fergusson regards as displaying the (1st) Pathán style at its period of greatest perfection, when the Hindu masons had learned to fit their exquisite minuteness of decoration to the forms of their foreign masters. This building is a square of 56½ feet, exterior measurement, the work being 11 feet thick. On each side there is a lofty doorway with a pointed arch, not a true horseshoe, but deriving some of that character from the arrangement of the pilasters from which it springs.

* *Vide infra*, p. 66. There was also a Saint, Kutab-ud-din Bakhtyárkákí, after whom the Mosque and Minár are by some believed to have been named.

The whole facade is covered with delicate chiselling, and the inner walls are decorated with a diaper pattern "of unrivalled excellence." The square form of the ground plan changes into the octagon from which the roof dome rises in a manner, says Mr. Fergusson, "more simply elegant and appropriate than any with which I am acquainted;" namely, by each corner forming a series of arched niches. The side-windows, of smaller size than the door, but similar shape, are closed with massive pierced marble screens, and the same material is freely used as a colouring variety to the stone which forms the substance of the building. The dome is a pure hemisphere. It may be doubted whether Indian Saracenic can show any specimen more beautiful, in a constructive point of view, than this. The dome has been found fault with as not high enough; but that depends on the point from which it is viewed. The side doors are much lower than those in front and rear; and this and similar expedients give the interior of this building its peculiar characteristic of symmetrical variety. The name of Álá-ud-din will be found sculptured over the inner archways in the spandrels.

The same monarch appears to have entertained the project of building a tower just double the size of the Kutab Minár on the opposite or northern side of the Mosque. It is believed that this work was begun in 1311 and stopped some time before the actual end of the reign, in consequence of a severe illness which disabled the King from public affairs, and from which he never recovered. The idea of beating the splendid tower of his predecessors by dint of mere size does no credit to Álá-ud-din's taste; and I do not know that the world has much cause for regret that this semi-insane project of a sickening despot was never carried into effect.

Shams-ud-din Altamsh. previously mentioned as the favourite slave who ruled after the death of his patron Kutab-ud-din Aibak, died in A.D. 1236, and his tomb, built by his son and daughter, is just at the north-west extremity of the Mosque. "Though small," says Fergusson, "it is one of the richest examples of Hindu art applied to Mahometan purposes that old Dehli affords; and is extremely beautiful, though the builders still display a certain degree of inaptness in fitting the details to their new uses." Remarking that the effect of the building is at present marred by the want of a roof, he concludes his description by noting that it is the oldest tomb known to exist in India. Here again we note the use of white marble to relieve the red sandstone, and we seem to observe the dawning of the art which afterwards led to such beautiful results in the application of inlaid colour on buildings at Agra. General Cunningham notes that there is a western niche in this building, as if it had been intended for use as a Mosque, and that the existence of a single stone of one of the circular cornices used in Hindu domes shows that it probably was once roofed by an overlapping vault of that description.

On the western wall will be observed a recess, as in the corresponding part of a regular Mosque. This feature also exists in the tomb of Nizámudin, and in others of even a later date. Another peculiarity of Altamsh's tomb is, that the arches are false, having no keystone or radiating voussoirs, a peculiarity that they share with the high entries to the Kutab-al-Islám, the outer walls of which moreover have square openings to the windows. All this shows dependence on Hindu workmen. Fifty or sixty years later, when the first decorated Pathán school was as its height, the quasi-horseshoe arch with a pointed apex was in full use, as seen at the Alái-Darwázá. The walls with which Álá-uddin flanked the fresh cloisters that he erected about the Kutab have similar openings, and they are also found in the remains known as "The Palace" of that monarch. It must have been in the long reign of that sumptuous parvenu Bulbun (*infra*, p. 63) that architecture arose among the Patháns and that the principles of the arch were mastered by them; though little or nothing is left of his own buildings, which are believed to have been at Kiloghari—near Humáyun's tomb.

ÁDHAM KHANS TOMB.

History relates that one Ádham Khán, apparently a bastard of the house of Timur, was sent, early in the reign of Akbar, to suppress an adherent of the house of Sur, by name Báz Báhádur. This leader's wife, Rupmati, was famous for her beauty and accomplishments, and a poetess of celebrity then, whose name is still in men's mouths. Ádham Khán having put Báz to flight, took possession of his chief town, Sarangpur, and ordered the lady to receive him. Being unable to refuse the conqueror, she ordered him to be admitted, but when he reached her apartment he found that she had arrayed herself in silk and gems, had unveiled her face, swallowed poison, and was cold and dead. Shortly after returning to the Court at Agra from this exploit the victorious general quarrelled with the foster-father of the young Emperor, whom he stabbed in the Diwán-i-Ám of Akbar's Palace. It was evening, but the Prince was roused, and came out of the private apartments behind. On the assassin coming towards him in what was perhaps an undecided attitude between menace and apology, Akbar knocked him down with his own fist, and then directed that he should be hurled from the terrace on which they stood. Tradition relates that this was done twice before the wretched man ceased to breathe. His mother died of grief a month later, and the Emperor buried them both in this spot. The tomb where they were laid is grand in its stern simplicity, and though, of course, chronologically Mughal, may be called a work of the third Pathán period ; more indeed resembling the style of the second, already encountered at Firozábád, and again to occur at Toghlakábád and the great tomb of Toghlak Sháh.

This building—which is large, well raised, and in excellent preservation—is fitted up as a European dwelling-house. Not far off, to the south-west, is the "Metcalfe House," a substantial and still more commodious dwelling, built round another mediæval sepulchre.

It may be noticed that the tomb of Ádham Khán is a curiosity on account of its belonging to Pathán school, though dating later than Humáyun's tomb and other early Moghul buildings. The same overlapping of styles characterises the Chini-ká-Rozá at Agra.

Captain Harcourt advises us to go to the Mausoleum of Sultán Ghori on the morning of the last day : and gives the following description of the building :

This lies to the west of the Kutab, some four miles off the road lying through Mábsudpor, the Mausoleum being in the village of Mallickpor Koyi, which is now deserted ; the wells in the neighbourhood being to this day perfectly dry. Sultán Ghori was the son of the Emperor Shams-ud-din Altamsh, who reigned from A.D. 1211 to A.D. 1236. The building is one of much interest, and worthy of visit ; it is principally composed of marble.

The chief interest is architectural, the building being an example of the first Pathán period.

TOGHLAKÁBÁD.

Turning eastward, the fine ruins of Toghlakábád will be found about four miles from the Kutab Bangalow. This almost cyclopean group of buildings, recalling one of the painters, Martin's grand architectural dreams, was built early in the fourteenth century by Toghlak Ghází Khán, a successful military adventurer, who overthrew the house of Khiliji and ascended the imperial throne at the epoch. The following animated description by General Cunningham contains almost all that need be said upon the present condition of this Castle:—

"The Fort of Toghlakábád may be described with tolerable accuracy as a half-hexagon in shape, with three faces of rather more than three-quarters of a mile in length each, and a base of one mile and-a-half, the whole circuit being only one furlong less than four miles. The Fort stands on a rocky height, and is built of massive blocks of stone, so large and heavy that they must have been quarried on the spot. The largest stone which I observed measured fourteen feet in length by two feet two inches, and one foot ten inches in breadth and thickness, and must have weighed rather more than six tons. The short faces to the north-west and east are protected by a deep ditch, and the long face to the south by a large sheet of water, which is held up by an embankment at the south-east corner. On this side the rock is scarped, and above it the main walls rise to a mean height of forty feet, with a parapet of seven feet, behind which rises an another wall of fifteen feet, the whole height above the low ground being upwards of nineteen feet. In the south-west angle is the citadel, which occupies about one-sixth of the area of the Fort, and contains the ruins of an extensive palace. The ramparts are raised as usual on a line of domed rooms, which rarely communicate with each other, and which no doubt formed the quarters of the troops that garrisoned the Fort. The walls slope rapidly inwards, even as much as those of Egyptian buildings. The rampart walls are pierced with loopholes, which serve also to give light and air to the soldiers' quarters. The parapets are pierced with low sloping loopholes, which command the foot of the wall, and are crowned with a line of rude battlements of solid stone, which are also provided with loopholes. The walls are built of large painly dressed stones, and there is no ornament of any kind; but the vast size, the great strength, and the visible solidity of the whole give to Toghlakábád an air of stern and massive grandeur, that is both striking and impressive. The Fort of Toghlakábád has thirteen gates, and there are three inner gates to the citadel; it contains seven tanks of water besides the ruins of several large buildings, as the Jamá Masjid and the Burj Munder. The upper part of the Fort is full of ruined houses, but the lower part appears as if it had never been fully inhabited."

It was commenced by the Emperor Toghlak Sháh about A.D. 1321, and was finished—at any rate, as much finished as it is now—by A.D. 1323. It may be added that the area is about equal to that of Sháhjahánábád, and that the interior is an open plain five miles in circumference; there is little to see within besides a well, cut in the solid rock to a depth of about 80 feet, and the ruins of the founder's Palace. He was killed by an accident,* supposed to have been contrived by his son, and buried in a striking situation about 300 yards in front of the principal gate of his unfinished city, of which indeed the tomb with its fortress may be said to form a sort of outwork. The work appears according to Tartar custom to have been planned and perhaps constructed in the lifetime of the person for whom it was intended. The following are Mr. Fergusson's remarks on this grand relic of irresponsible power: — "When the stern old warrior Toghlak Sháh (1321) founded the new Dehli, which still bears his name, he built himself a tomb, not in a garden as was usually the case, but in a strongly fortified citadel in the middle of an artificial lake. The sloping walls and almost Egyptian solidity of this Mausoleum, combined with the bold massive towers of the fortifications that surround it, form a picture of a warrior's tomb unrivalled anywhere, and a singular contrast to the elegant and luxurious garden tombs of the more settled and peaceful dynasties that succeeded."

It is noted by Cunningham that the same Emperor built himself another tomb in something of a similar style in the Fort of Multán, but considerably larger, which he afterwards gave to a holy man of the day. The tomb at Dehli is moreover of better materials than its precursor, being entirely of stone finely ornamented with white marble. It is surrounded by a pentagonal outwork, connected with the fortress by a causeway 600 feet long, supported on 27 arches. The tomb itself is a square of 61½ feet exteriorly, the walls being 21½ feet thick, and 38½ feet high, with a slope of 7½ feet from top to bottom. The total height to the top of the domed roof is 70 feet, and the pinnacle is 10 feet more, and each of the four sides has a lofty doorway with a pointed arch, fretted on the

* *Vide* Appendix D.

outer edge. The decorations are produced by the admixture of white marble above referred to, and are probably the precursors of the inlayings which afterwards came to form such an important feature of Hindustáni architecture. Within are three tombs said to be those of the old King, his wife, and his son and successor; the latter is believed to contain the singular collection of vouchers for pardon which the pious care of the good Emperor Firoz Sháh, who succeeded him, provided for the dead hand to pick up and arise with on the day of judgment. Here is an account of the transaction taken from the words of Firoz himself:—

"I have taken pains to discover the surviving relations of all persons who suffered from the wrath of my late Lord; and having pensioned and provided for them, and for those who had been maimed by order of the late Sultán, have caused them to execute deeds, declaring their satisfaction, duly witnessed; these being placed in a chest have been deposited at the head of the tomb of the said Sultán in the hope that God of his infinite mercy will take compassion on my departed friend."

The Emperor thus accredited to the Mercy-seat of Divine Omnipotence was probably the maddest monster of cruelty that ever sat on a throne. He has earned an infamous immortality as the *Khuni Sultán*, or "Bloody Lord," by which title he is still known in popular tradition. A man may be stronger than the people for a time, but the people never dies.* The small Fort of *Adilábád*, near the south-east corner of Toghlakábád, is the only complete building of this tyrant, who died in 1351. His Fort of *Jehán Paná*, now a ruin, must be mentioned more in detail.

JAHANPANA.

According to Captain Harcourt's Diary, our pilgrimage is is now at an end; but before leaving the neighbourhood of the Kutab, the lover of antiquity may find work for another pleasant day. North-east of the Kutab ground will be found the remains of Muhammad Toglak's fortification, known by the name *Jehán Paná*, or "world's asylum," a very alluring title, probably not fulfilled in the experience of the population. The suburbs of old Dehli in this direction having been plundered during incursions of Moghul invaders during the

---

* *Vide infra*, Historical Note.

reign of Alá-ud-din, their unprotected state is regarded by Cunningham as having justified the vast outlay which their fortification involved. The north-west wall is stated by the same authority to be 1½ mile long, the east wall ½, the south 2 miles; the whole length of the *enceinte* being five miles, or somewhat more than the circuit of Rái Pithorá's Fort at the Kutab. There were, it is recorded, thirteen gates, six to the north and seven to the south. A considerable amount of wall is still standing in the last-named direction.

SIRI.

Sultán Álá-ud-din founded the city of Siri to the north-east of the Kutab, as it were an off-shoot of the old Dilli. In this reign the Moghuls under Janghiz Khán invaded India in A.D. 1303, and advanced on Álá-ud-din. The latter intrenched himself apparently at Siri (now Sháhpore), and on the sudden retreat of the Moghuls, caused a palace to be built on the spot where his camp had been. "On this side," says General Cunningham, "the suburbs of the old Dilli extended for a considerable distance. We know also that they were without walls, because the Moghuls plundered them during their stay, and because they were afterwards enclosed by Muhammad Toghlak, when they received the separate name of Jehán Panná.* Immediately in front of these suburbs, and facing towards the enemy, is the old ruined Fort of Sháhpore, and inside the west half of this Fort there still exist the remains of a very extensive palace. This palace I believe to be the celebrated Kasr-Hazár-Situn, or palace of the thousand pillars, which Álá-ud-din built on the spot where he had intrenched himself. This palace was called Hazár Minár, or thousand minarets." "Siri," adds General Cunningham, "cannot be identified with the citadel that surrounds the Kutab Minár, for the walls of Siri were pulled down and the material removed by Sher Sháh (between A.D. 1540 and 1545), while the walls of the Kutab Minár citadel are still standing. And further, it seems almost certain that Sháhpore must be Siri, because of its vicinity to the new

* Ibn Batuta states that Muhammad intended to join Dehli, Siri, Jehán Paná, and Toghlakábád in one fortification, but was deterred by the cost. This was before he removed all the inhabitants to the Deccan.

site of Sher Sháh's Fort, for it is hardly possible to believe that the King would have brought his building stones from the Kutab Minár, a distance of seven miles, when he could have obtained them from Sháhpore, which is only half the distance. That he did obtain his materials from the latter place, and not from the former, may be regarded as almost certain, for the very sufficient reason that the walls of Sháhpore have actually been removed, while those of the Kutab citadel are still standing."

This was the Dehli of Tamerlane, described in the memoirs of that monarch known as the *Tuzuk-i-Timur;* and consisted of three conjoined cities, like Westminster, London, and the Borough. The following quaint account of the place is given by the invader:—

"When my mind was no longer occupied with the destruction of the people of Dehli, I took a ride round the cities. Siri is a round city; its buildings are lofty, surrounded by strong fortifications of stone and brick; old Dehli has a similar fort, but larger. From one to another—a considerable distance—runs a strong wall built of stone and cement, the part called Jehán Paná is in the centre of the inhabited area. The fortifications of the three cities have thirty gates, of which Jehán Paná has thirteen, Siri seven, and old Dehli ten." —[Abstracted from Elliot, in *Dowson's History of India*, Vol. III.]

Siri was destroyed by the Interrex Sher Sháh, in order that the materials might be worked into structures of his own.

LOCALITIES OF THE SIEGE OF DEHLI, 1857.

Having examined all the chief antiquarian objects for which Dehli is renowned, the visitor may still have time to go over the scenes of later events. The taking of Dehli in 1857 was perhaps a greater feat of arms than many which are more talked of; and is one that, without disparagement to native valour, may be truly said to have been impossible except between Europeans and Asiatics. Here was an *enceinte* of more than five miles, with curtains, bastions, gates, ditch, counterscarp, and glacis, all designed and partly carried out by British Engineers, with a strong arsenal and a complete park of heavy guns, taken by a handful of men (of whom indeed a portion were natives) at the first serious assault. The performances of Alexander and Xenophon are outdone by this marvellous achievement; and it is but natural that the visitor should linger over the places that testify of it, even with more interest because of its nearness to his own time, and in many cases, because of his own proper patriotism.

It will be remembered that in the description of the City (p. 25) the circuit of the walls was stated (on the authority of Captain Harcourt) to be five and-a-half miles.

In the anarchy that followed the absence, and finally, the death of the next Emperor, Aurungzeb, these walls probably received but little attention; and in 1804, when Holkár was at Mattrá, confronting the victorious Lake in his cantonments at Agra, the defences of Dehli were nothing but "dilapidated works and ruinous ramparts." But when Holkár, leaving his camp standing, made a rush upon Dehli, thinking to carry off the Emperor by a *coup de main*, there were those within, led by Sir David Ochterlony, who made a very different defence of bad walls to what was made of the same walls in their restored condition half a century later. The garrison was too small to allow of any reliefs, and they had to take their meals, each man at his post, upon the battlements: but the besieging force of 20,000 men, with one hundred pieces of cannon, beleaguered them in vain for nine whole days, after which the baffled tiger withdrew from his unsuccessful spring. The walls were afterwards repaired, and the complete restoration of the masonry had only been brought to a conclusion a few months before the outbreak of 11th May, 1857. Early on the morning of that day the revolted troopers of the 3rd Bengal Cavalry, who had escaped chastisement at Meerut, trotted across the bridge-of-boats, and entered the city. The whole of the garrison, being natives, joined them, and the work of villainy began. Mr. Simon Fraser, the Resident, Captain Douglas, Commanding the Palace Guard, with the Chaplain and his daughter, were killed at the main gate of the citadel; Colonel Ripley and other Officers of the 74th N. I. were pistolled in front of their own men, standing passive; the Magazine was invested: and the Europeans, men, women, children, chased over the walls of the city, to be shot down, or driven to the temporary shelter of the Flag Staff Tower, as might be their fate. The explosion of the Magazine by Willoughby and Forrest, and the escape of many of the defenders, who, fording the broad Jamná, joined the main stream of refugees on the other side, and in many instances got off safely to Meerut are events well-known and hardly belonging to our subject.

This was the opportunity of the powers of evil; and no one knows the full extent of the horrors that ensued in the long peaceful City of the Moghul. But the tables were to be turned, though at first but slowly. Victorious at *Badli-ki-Sarai*, the small avenging force found themselves on the evening of the 8th June face to face with all that the tourist of to-day sees basking in the beautiful winter sunshine from Hindu Rao's house. With their left on the river and their right on Kishanganj and the Sabzi Mundi gardens, the assailants were confronted by the northern angle of the fortifications, hardly extending from the Water Bastion to the Cábul Gate; investment was necessarily impossible. Here, during the heat of June, and the rotting reek of the ensuing monsoon, constantly reinforced by driblets (sent by the wise and strong rulers of the Panjáb) barely replacing the loss of sickness and of four-and-twenty desperate sorties by the besieged, did our handful of heroes maintain their perilous guard. At the time of the assault there were 2,500 men sick.

At length arrived John Lawrence's last remnant of troops, and—ten thousand in one—the peerless John Nicholson. "Now or never" was the motto brought down from his Chief by the great frontier soldier; and the whole force, inspired by the situation, at once prepared for their momentous undertaking. It was indeed now or never. The tension of the situation was become extreme, not only in the Panjáb, but in the whole Peninsula; and it was in the hands of less than 7,000 men of all arms to turn the doubtful scale one way or the other.

From the 8th to the 13th September the gunners of England beat incessantly upon the northern walls. Night and day went on the work of destruction from fifty guns of position. In the Kudsia garden on the river bank Tombs had a battery of ten mortars; another batterry under Scott being placed at the Custom-house. Ten guns in front played on the Moree and Cashmere Bastions from a distance of 700 yards under the able command of Major Brind. Other batteries were roaring from the Residency and from Hindu Rao's house on the top of the ridge. On the evening of the 13th the Engineer Officers reported two practicable breaches, one at the Cashmere Bastion, the other by the Water Gate; these stormed and the Cashmere Gate held by a third column, due provision being made for support on the rear and right flank, and all the columns might meet victorious at the barbican of the Palace within. As the day broke on the following morning, the incessant roar of the past week came to a sudden and ominous pause; the 60th Rifles, according to previous arrangement, sprang out with a cheer to cover the advance, and Salkeld and Home, of the Bengal Engineers, stepped forward with Non-Commissioned Officers, bugler, powder-carriers, to blow in the Cashmere Gate. The scene that followed is thus described by Colonel Medley, R.E., an eye-witness: "Followed by the storming party, 150 strong, Home and his party reached the outer gate almost unseen. With difficulty they crossed the ditch, and having laid their bags retired unharmed. It was now Salkeld's turn. He also advanced with four other bags of powder and lighted portfire, but the enemy had seen the smallness of the party and the object of their approach. A deadly fire was poured upon the little band from the open wicket not ten feet distant. Salkeld laid his bags, but was shot through the arm and leg, and fell back on the bridge, *handing the portfire to Sergeant Burgess, bidding him light the fuse. Burgess was instantly shot dead in the attempt. Sergeant Carmichael then advanced, took up the portfire, and succeeded in the attempt, but immediately fell mortally wounded. Sergeant Smith, seeing him fall, advanced at a run*, but finding that the fuse was already burning threw himself into the ditch. . . . . In another moment a terrific explosion shattered the massive gate, the bugle sounded the advance, and then with a loud cheer the storming party was in the gateway, and in a few minutes more the Cashmere Gate and Main Guard were once more in our hands."

It may be doubted whether a finer display of soldiership was ever made than that recorded in the simple lines above italicised. All the survivors were recommended for the Victoria Cross, but Salkeld died of his wounds; and it is melancholy to add that Home, after coming scatheless out of that ordeal, met his death in "a petty fortress" a few weeks later.

The progress of the assault is matter of military history. The saddest interest that attaches to it is connected with the fate of General Nicholson, of whom the Panjáb Government recorded that but for him Dehli would not have fallen. As bold in action as wise in council, this born soldier, emerging from a *catcherry*, achieved immortality in dying at the age of 35. After leading his column over the breach by the side of the Cashmere Gate he re-formed his men (detachments from the 75th, the 1st Fusiliers,* and the 2nd Punjábees) by

* Subsequently the 101st R. B. F.

the Main Guard. Turning to the right by the narrow lane behind the city-walls, Nicholson next proceeded to open a way parallel with the ramparts, and had already captured the Cábul Gate. In proceeding towards the Burn bastion a check was experienced from a breastwork and one gun on the ramparts; and it was in waving on the men against this obstacle, his fine form in advance, conspicuously displayed to the fire of countless enfilading muskets from the windows that lined the lane, that he received his mortal wound and was borne to the rear. Uttering words of valorous counsel from his pallet, the hero died; but his spirit lived among the force in all ranks; and on the fifth day the whole vast area of the city was in the hands of Sir Archdale Wilson.* The trial and exile of the King and the peaceable reorganisation of civil order followed shortly; and there is little now to remind the visitor of those brave days, save the monument of Nicholson, and the memorial column, 110 feet in height, which stands on a commanding point of the Ridge, upon the site once occupied by one of the breaching Batteries. This monument commemorates the deeds of the gallant captors of Dehli, and was erected by the subscriptions of the survivors, supplemented by aid from the Government. The total cost is stated by Harcourt to have amounted to 22,400 rupees. There is a winding stair within, and a fine view from the top of all the scenes of the siege.

HISTORICAL NOTE.

The note appended to the *Agra Guide* gives historical memoranda regarding those Moghul rulers with whom the buildings at Agra are chiefly connected. In the present note will be found a similar account of their Patháns predecessors to whose memory the neighbourhood of Dehli has so many splendid monuments.

We have already seen that there is a probability of some remains near the Kutab dating from a period antecedent by a few years to the Christian era. The edicts of Asoká indeed, on Firoz Sháh's *Lat*, are older still, but this pillar (*vide supra*, p. 29) does not appear to have been originally erected in the Dehli district; and the possible settlement of the Pándu brothers at Indráprasthá has left no mark behind.

What little is known of the early Hindu dynasties of Dehli

* The total loss in this attack was no less than 66 officers and 1,100 men.

will be found in the Archæologic Reports of General Cunningham so often drawn upon in the preceding pages. Their remains are—the Iron Pillar, the columns of the great Mosque, and the fortifications of Lálkot and the adjacent works.

The authentic history of Dehli can hardly be said to begin before the end of the twelfth century from Christ, when Shahábud-din Ghori, otherwise known as Muhammad Bin Sám, was sent against the then ruling Chaubáns of Northern India. In 1193 the Mahomedans were routed by Pirthi Ráj—or Rái Pithorá—on the plain of Thanesar, but two years later they returned with irresistible force, and overthrew the Rájputs near the same ground. Bin Sám left a favorite follower, Kutab-ud-din Aibak, to administer the affairs of Hindustán, but returned in person shortly after, leaving his brother as sole monarch at Ghazni. He died in a campaign in the Panjáb in 1206, and Kutab-ud-din succeeded to the throne of Dehli. It was in the reign of this monarch that the Kutab Minár was commenced, and was adorned with a scroll commemorative of his deceased patron. This is the beginning of what has been called "The Slave Dynasty," in reference to the fact that these monarchs were often succeeded by favorite slaves. The most famous of them are:—

Shams-ud-din Altamsh, 1211—1236.

In his reign the Kutab Minár was first completed; he also built the earlier part of the *Butkhánna*, or great pillared cloisters of the Kutab Mosque—A.D. 1220—and the college attached to which is the building where he himself was afterwards buried.

After a variety of short reigns, mostly ending in the assassination of the sovereign by some profligate courtier, the throne was ascended in 1246 by Nasir-ud-din. This monarch was little better than a recluse; but he had the good sense to leave the conduct of affairs to an able Minister, and died in his bed without heirs, after a tranquil reign of twenty years.

The minister, Balban, succeeded without a contest, A.D. 1265-6. He had originally been one of the band of Turk slaves known as "The Forty," who had become enormously powerful under the weak administrations that had long prevailed. The historian Barni, who had conversed with the contemporaries of this ruler, relates that, for the twenty-two years that Balban reigned, he maintained the dignity of his throne in unsurpassable splendour, and was never seen by his most confidential attendants otherwise than in full dress! "He never allowed any one to joke in his presence, nor did he permit any one in his court to laugh." "No one ever dared to recommend for employment any person of low position or extraction." This magnificent *parvenu* seems really to have been an efficient ruler; he made some startling examples amongst his own friends who had misconducted themselves, and he put the army on so sound a footing that Bengál was subdued and the Moghul invasion rolled back. Eventually, however, he lost his favourite son in battle against the Moghuls, who at the same time took prisoner the Poe Khusru (*vide supra*, p. 36), who was not liberated till his friends had paid a heavy ransom for him. Balban died of a broken heart, and was succeeded by his grandson Kái Kobád in A.D. 1286-7.

The dissolute habits of this monarch soon led to his being seized by paralysis, in which state he was kicked to death in his bed by a dissatisfied slave, and the Slave dynasty brought to an end.

The next line of Dehli Kings were a Pathán race, called Khilji; the first of whom, Jalál-ud-dín, ascended the throne in 1289. He was a mild ruler, and the country suffered much, both from internal broils and from Moghul irruptions during his reign. He eventually lost the confidence of his subjects and kindred, and was murdered in open day by his nephew and son-in-law Álá-ud-din.

Álá-ud-din Khilji became King in 1296. In his reign the famous Aulia adventurer Nizámudin (*supra*, p. 35) came to India. The reign lasted twenty years, and was at first distinguished by great activity in the way of architecture. We learned from the prose works of Khusru that the Mosque at the Kutab was completed by building beyond the old gates and courts a fourth [court] with high pillars, and upon the surface of the stones were engraved verses of the Korán (*vide supra*, p. 47). Álá-ud-din also undertook to outstrip the lofty *Maziná* of the Mosque, the Kutab Minár, intending, it is said, to double all the proportions. This is the unfinished basement described above (p. 51). He demolished the remains of Hindu temples that his predecessors had spared, and sprinkled the walls of the outer works with the blood of "some thousands of goat-bearded Moghuls," whom he "sacrificed" for the purpose. He appears to have been a blunt soldier, a little disposed to pride himself on his ignorance of law and learning, but having a keen sense of the dangers of Moghul invasion and of the necessity of guarding against it. It was with this object that he built the Fort of Siri (*supra*, p. 57) and fortified other places on the road of the invaders, which generally led by Multán, Depálpur, and

Lahore. His principal commander was Gházi Málik, who afterwards became King under the title of Mohamad Toghlak. The King, however, had more confidence in a companion of his profligacy called Málik Náib Káfur; and he appears to have paid the price of his carelessness by losing his life during an attack of dropsy, in which his mind failed, until his sufferings were put an end to by the unworthy favourite. Málik Káfur tried to carry on the Government, but he was in his turn assassinated, and, after a period of confusion in which the Hindus held Dehli and the neighbourhood for five months, the sceptre fell into the hands of Gházi Málik Gháyas-ud-din, Mohamad Toghlak, who ascended the throne in the palace at Siri in 1320 A.D. The capital was forthwith removed to the fortified city called Toghlakábád. Mr. Wheeler (*Hist. of India*, IV., i.) thinks that this was a soldierly measure, by which the new Emperor guarded himself against a further Hindu revival. His brief administration was what might have been expected from his apprenticeship, that of an honest and able soldier, but he perished by the contrivance of his son Junáh Khán (Appx. D.), having only ruled five years.

Junáh assumed the throne in his father's Fort of Toghlakábád (*supra*, p. 54) by the title of Mohamad-ibn-Toghlak Sháh. This is the prince described above by his more popular title of "Bloody Lord," and he is chiefly remarkable as a combination of literature without religion, and abundant accomplishments and ability with no tincture of the humanity that usually accompanies such gifts. Barni, who knew him well, records some of his excusatory yet menacing language. Famine fell on Dehli, which the King accordingly deserted, driving the population to Deogir, the same place as what was hereafter known as Daulutábád, near Ellorá, in what is now the Nizám's country.

He then tried to re-populate Dehli from places in the neighbourhood. By this and other wilful projects he raised general discontent, which he tried to put down with unexampled violence. "I have no pleasure," he said, "in revolts, though people will say 'tis my own conduct caused them. I am not to be turned from my system of punishment either by revolts or reasonings. . . . . . I visit with chastisement upon presumption of rebellious designs, and I punish with death the most trifling acts of contumacy. And this I will do until I die." This bewildered tyrant contemplated abdication later in his reign, "I am angry with my subjects," he told Barni in a conversation shortly before the end of his reign; "no treatment of mine does any good.

My remedy is the sword . . . so that a cure may be effected by suffering. The more I chastise the more they rebel." Yet he was never personally molested and died a natural death, in the full exercise of the power he had so long abused, to be peacefully succeeded by his cousin in 1350.

Firoz Sháh, one of the best men of that dark time, was in Sindh when the late King expired. After capturing an imbecile opponent he proceeded to Dehli, where he occupied a long reign in the most praiseworthy efforts to protect his people and to give them employment in beautifying the adjacent cities and in restoring the monuments of his predecessors. In the modest and pious sketch of his own exploits which he left behind him, this beneficent ruler expressly states that he gave the restoration of these buildings the priority over his own works, an instance of self-denial rare indeed among Asiatic rulers. He introduced their names into the public Litanies at the Mosques, and carried his zeal for the spiritual welfare of his own patron and immediate predecessor so far as to provide him in his grave with vouchers for the Great Audit A list of his various works would be tedious, especially as many of them have ceased to exist. Most of those which are still extant are referred to in the preceding pages, and others of a less interesting character lie scattered between Nizámudin's tomb and the neighbourhood of the Kutab, such as the *Jamát Kháná** Mosque, and the tank and tomb at *Hauz Khás*.

In the contemporary narrative of Áfif it is stated that the city of Firoz contained eighteen townships, and that from Indurpat to the Khusk Shikár on the ridge, a distance of five kos, all was built on. The city contained eight public Mosques and one private Chapel, and the public Mosques accommodated each, on an average, 10,000 worshippers. If this is to be taken as an index of the population, it will be seen that the city must, in its palmiest days, have contained at least double the population estimated by Cunningham, or say, 350,000 souls, each worshipper being taken as a householder.

In the anarchy that ensued upon the abdication of Firoz occurred the most terrible of all the Moghul incursions, that of Timur the Lame, whose description of the three cities of old Dehli has already been extracted (*supra*, p. 58). He also describes in his memoirs the Hauz (water-tomb) of that monarch, and a Mosque with which he was so much pleased

* *Vide supra*, p. 36.

that he carried back the sons of the builders to erect a similar place of worship in Samárcand.

This was at the end of the 14th century; and the history of Dehli from this time to the invasion and conquest of Hindustán by Timur's descendant, Bábar, a century and-a-quarter later, is of little archæological interest. The domains of the rulers of Dehli shrank to the dimensions of a private estate, and it was not till the rise of the Lodi dynasty (a brief Pathán race) that a dim crepuscular grandeur arose, which was illustrated by the third, or decorated order of Pathán Architecture. The finest specimen of the Lodi period is the tomb of Sikandar Sháh, referred to in page 41, and that was perhaps not built by the Lodi Kings, but by their still more brief-termed successors the Patháns of the race of Sur. A true Lodi building exists at Roshan Chirágh, the tomb of Behlol, who died in 1488. Some remains of his successor Sikandar are thought to have existed in the Agra Fort, but they cannot now be traced. There is also a theory which has not yet been either completely established or completely overthrown that the tomb of Akbar's wife at Sikandra was originally a *báradari* of the time of this monarch.

APPENDIX A.

THE ELEPHANT STATUES.

These sculptures have fallen into a fragmentary state. One of them has lately been, rather clumsily, restored; but there can be little doubt but that both once stood outside what, from the description, was not the "Dehli Gate" or the main barbican of the Palace, but rather, as Mr. Carr-Setphen thinks, the *Nakarkhána* (Music Gate) or the Háthi Pul. Bernier in 1663 saw them, and was told that they were the representation of two Chiefs of Chittor, Jáymal and Fatthá, who had been conquered and slain by Akbar, and that this monarch put the statues up in admiration of their prowess. The riders are not now mounted. One of the elephants, indeed, seems to have totally disappeared, and the other stands in the public garden, with an inscription that does not connect it with the occasion of Chittor. But the "resolute riders" are to be found in the verandah of the museum, and, even in their decay, well sustain the epithet of Bernier. Two other mutilated *torsos*, on the same semi-colossal scale, are by them, and are supposed to have represented the Mahouts, or drivers, who guided the elephants in battle. Francklin (the author of *Sháh Alam*), who visited Dehli in 1793, ascertained that these images had been removed by Aurungzeb, as savouring too much of idolatry. They were discovered about 1863, buried among some rubbish inside the Fort. General Cunningham, accepting Bernier's account of these figures, concludes that they were originally placed by Akbar in front of the River Gate of the Agra Fort, and that they are mentioned in the Áyin as "two elephants with their riders, at the Eastern Gate," where they stood until removed by his grandson to adorn the new Palace at Dehli. He describes them as follows:—

"The statues of Jáymal and Pattá are simply valuable as works of art, as they are, perpaps, the only portrait statues that have been erected in India for many centuries. They are made of red sandstone, and are of life-size, while the huge elephants on which they sit are of black marble, and the housings are decorated with white and yellow marbles."

They were probably moved to Delhi from Agra in the time of Sháhjahán, but it is not so clear how and when they were first erected.

Bernier's, says General Cunningham, is the first mention of these statues. What then is to be made of this passage in Finch's description of the Agra Fort, with Purchas' marginal note?—

"To the castle are four gates, one to the north, by which you passe to a Rampire with great peeces, another west to the *Bázár*, called the *Cicherry* Gate, within which, over against the great gate, is the *Cazi*, his seat of Chief Justice in matters of law, and by it two or three mortars very great (some three foot in the bore and fifteen long) of cast brasse . . . . Beyond these two gates you passe a second gate, over which are two *Rájáws* in stone,* who were slain in the King's Darbár before the King's eyes, for being over-bold in speech, they selling their lives bravely, in remembrance of which they are here placed. Passing this gate, you enter into a fair street, with houses and munition all along in both sides. At the end of this street being a quarter of a mile, you come to the third gate, which leads to the King's Darbár, always chained, all men, but the King and his children, there alighting. This gate is to the south, called *Acăbár Drowázá*. . . . . . .

"The fourth gate is to the river, called the *Dersane*, leading into a fair Court extending along the river, in which the King looks forth every morning at sun-rising, which he salutes, and then his Nobles resort to their *Tessillam*.† Right under the place where he looks out, is a kind of scaffold, whereon his Nobles stand, but the *Addis* with others await below in the Court. Here also every noone he looketh forth to behold *Tamáshâh*, or fighting of Elephants, Lyons, Buffles, killing of Deare with Leopards; which is a custom on every day of the weeke, Sunday excepted, on which is no fighting; but Tuesday, on the contrary, is a day of blood, both of fighting beasts, and justiced men, the King judging and seeing execution. To returne to the third gate, within it you enter into a spacious Court with *Atrecanna's* round-about-like shops and open halls, wherein his Captains, according to their degrees, keep

* It is said that they were two brothers, Rájputs, tutors to a Prince, their nephew, whom the King demanded of them. They refused, and were committed; but drew on the officers, slew twelve, and at last, by multitudes oppressing, were slain, and here have elephants of stone and themselves figured.—*Purchas' note.*

† A posture of humiliation.—*Purchas.*

their seventh day Chockees. A little further you enter within a rayle, into a more inward Court, within which none but the King's *Addis*, and men of sort are admitted, under paine of smacking by the Porters' Cudgels, which lay on loud without respect of persons."*—*Purchas, B. IV, C. 4, S. VI.*, p. 439.

[Much of this account may apply to features that were changed afterwards (*vide* account of the Palaces in the *Handbook to Agra*), but some of the apparent confusion will be got rid of if we understand the gates originally called 1st and 2nd to have been regarded as one, *a double*, gate; as in fact is still the case. The 3rd gate is then seen to have been rightly called "the 2nd," and this was the entrance to the street since known as *Mina Bázár*, which, previous to British Military precautions, formed the approach to the *Ám-Khás* and the rest of the Palace. The "3rd" gate is the gate opening on the great Court of the Armoury, or *Ám-Khás*; and the 4th is the now disused water-gate, which does not open upon the strand but faces eastward; and had a bit of *glacis* extended before it, before the outer wall and the moat were added on the river-face, probably in the time of Aurungzeb, or late in the reign of his predecessor. The statues, therefore, were at the entrance, not of the Fort, but of the Palace, and were distinctly seen by Finch, if not by Hawkins.

The "Addis" are *Ahdis*, "the single men," a sort of gentlemen-cadets waiting for their commissions, and not required to do sentry or fatigue-duty. There was a corresponding class in the old French *Maison du Roy*, known as *Exempts*, whence we have to this day in England the royal "*Exons* of the guard." The person of the sovereign was the post of these men-at-arms; and parades of them took place in the *Ám-Khás* of Agra and Dehli.]

Finch himself, it is true, says nothing about elephants; but he mentions Rájás, not defenders of Chittor, but turbulent men slain in Darbár (as in the later story of Amar Singh). The allusion probably is to the three sons of Akhiráj, son of Akbar's brother-in-law Rájáh Bhagwán Dás of Jaipur, killed in a fight arising out of a tumult caused by themselves in the Palace (*Memoirs of Jahángir*, p. 12, quoted by Prof. Blochmann, *Cal. Rev.*, CIX, 1331). And Purchas, who died in 1628, must evidently have had good authority for saying that the Rájás were on elephants. But by no possibility can the

* This is the *Am-Khás*, divided, it would seem, in those days into an outer and inner Court. Hawkins speaks with pride of his being called within the 'red rail.'

situation ascribed to them be understood as "in front of the river gate." The river gate was evidently the *Dersane Drowázá*, in front of which was the area in which beast-fights and executions took place; but the gate of the elephant-statues was either the *Hathia-Pul* (as the name would suggest), or the inner entrance to the Palace; the two gates first mentioned being the two-fold gates of the great barbican still standing, by which one enters from the Jamá Masjid. As to Bernier, his information was later than Finch's by half a century; and as he was wrong in calling Jáymal the Rájá of Chittor, he may have equally been misled in supposing that Chittor and the statues had any connection whatever. It is curious that the Rájput bards are silent on the subject. The Akbarnámá is also silent as to the statues, though it describes the deaths of Pattá (or Fattá) and Jáymal. The name of the gate is apparently a hint as to where the elephants were placed; fronting or flanking the entrance to the Palace in the Fort which bears the name "Hathia-Pul," or Elephant-Gateway. But *when* they were erected or *whom* they commemorate cannot be regarded as conclusively settled. They are mentioned by de Laet (whose *India Vera* was published in 1631) in his usual inaccurate way:—

"This was a very great victory; and in memory of it, the King caused two elephants to be carved, Tyimal Patthá sitting on one, and one of his chief generals on the other; and caused them to be placed one on each side of the Fort at Agra."

I may add that there is internal evidence that de Laet (who wrote in Europe) got some of his information from Finch, as will be plain to any one who will compare the descriptions by the two writers, especially of Fattehpur-Sikri, and of the "Dehli" of that day—*Puráná Killá*.

It is easy, in the Dutch writer's—to us at least—unphonetic spelling to see that he has made Jáymal and Fattá into one person; they are still spoken of without the copula in popular idiom, sounding, to an inexperienced ear, like one word.

It may perhaps be suspected from these extracts that Purchas and Finch, the earliest authorities to whom the mention of these statues has been traced, are, after all, right in their account of the origin of the mysterious monuments. If so, it may be that the sculptures were ordered by Jahángir in a freak of remorse for the massacre of his kinsmen, and that other names were given them afterwards to divert attention from the scandal by connecting them with the glorious victory of Chittor.

APPENDIX B.

THE BRINGING OF THE PILLARS.

Removal of the Minára-i-Zarin.—" Khizrabad is ninety kos from Dehli, in the vicinity of the hills. When the Sultán visited that district, and saw the column in the village of Tobrá, he resolved to remove it to Dehli, and there erect it as a memorial to future generations. After thinking over the best means of lowering the column, orders were issued commanding the attendance of all the people dwelling in the neighbourhood, within and without the Doab, and all soldiers, both horse and foot. They were ordered to bring all implements and materials suitable for the work. Directions were issued for bringing parcels of the Cotton of the Semal (silk cotton tree). Quantities of this silk cotton were placed round the column, and when the earth at its base was removed, it fell gently over on the bed prepared for it. The cotton was then removed by degrees, and after some days the pillar lay safe upon the ground. When the foundations of the pillar were examined, a large square stone was found as a base, which also was taken out. The pillar was then encased from top to bottom in reeds and ram skins, so that no damage might accrue to it. A carriage, with forty-two wheels, was constructed, and ropes were attached to each wheel. Thousands of men hauled at every rope, and after great labour and difficulty the pillar was raised on to the carriage. A strong rope was fastened to each wheel, and 200 men pulled at each of these ropes. By the simultaneous exertions of so many thousand men the carriage was moved, and was brought to the banks of the Jamná. Here the Sultán came to meet it. A number of large boats had been collected, some of which could carry 5,000 and 7,000 maunds of grain, and the least of them 2,000 maunds.

The column was very ingeniously transferred to these boats, and was then conducted to Firozábád, where it was landed and conveyed into the Kushk with infinite labour and skill."

Account of the raising of the Obelisk.—" At this time the author of the book was twelve years of age, and a pupil of the respected Murkhán. When the pillar was brought to the place a building was commenced for its reception, near the Jamá Masjid, and the most skilful architects were employed. It was constructed of stone and chunam, and consisted of several stages or steps (poshish). When a step was finished, the column was raised on to it, another step was then built, and the pillar was again raised, and so on in succession until it reached the intended height.

"On arriving at this stage, other contrivances had to be devised to place it in an erect position. Ropes of great thickness were obtained, and windlasses were placed on each of the six stages of the base. The ends of the ropes were fastened to the top of the pillar, and the other ends passed over the windlasses, which were firmly secured with many fastenings. The wheels were then turned, and the column was raised about half a gaz. Logs of wood and bags of cotton were then placed under it to prevent its sinking again. In this way, by degrees, and in the course of several days, the column was raised to the perpendicular. Large beams were then placed round it as shores, until quite a cage of scaffolding was formed. It was thus secured in an upright position, straight as an arrow, without the smallest deviation from the perpendicular. The square stone before spoken of was placed under the pillar. After it was raised, some ornamental friezes of black and white stone were placed round its two Capitals (do-sáz-i-án), and over these there was raised a gilded copper cupola, called in Hindi Khalás. The height of the obelisk was thirty-two gaz; eight gaz was sunk in its pedestal, and twenty-four gaz was visible. On the base of the obelisk there were engraved several lines of writing in Hindi characters. Many Brahmans and Hindu devotees were invited to read them, but no one was able. It is said that certain infidel Hindus interpreted them as stating that no one should be able to remove the obelisk from its place till there should arise in the latter days a Mahamadan King named Sultán Firoz, &c., &c.

Erection of the other Obelisk in the Kushk Shikár.—"This obelisk stood in the vicinity of the Town of Meerut, in the Doab, and was somewhat smaller than the *Minára-i-Zarin.* This also was removed by Sultán Firoz, with similar skill and labour, and was re-erected on a hill in the *Kushk Shikár* (amid great feasting and rejoicing). After the erection of the pillar a large town sprang up, and the Kháns and Máliks of the Court built houses there. Every great King took care during his reign to set up some lasting memorial of his power. So Sultán Shams-u-din Altamsh raised the large pillar in the Masjid-i-jamá at old Dehli, the history of which is well-known.*

"In these days, in the year 801 H. (1399 A.D.) Amir Timur, of Khorásán, has marched into India, and by the will of fate has subdued the empire of Hindustán. During his stay of some days in Dehli he inspected all the monuments of former Kings, and among them these two obelisks, when he declared that in all the countries he had traversed he had never seen any monuments comparable to these."—*Shams-i-Siráj Afif, quoted in Elliot's History of India by Dowson, Vol. III.*

* This is the Kutab Minár.

APPENDIX C.

The following general description of the edicts of Asoká is taken from the work of a learned Hindu :—

"Some include more and some less : they are standing at Dilli (Dehli), Pryág (Alláhábád), and Bakrá ; also in Sirhut near Rádhia, and Mathia. . . . The summary of the fourteen articles in brief is—(1) the preservation of animal life ; (2) extension of cultivation ; (3) quinquennial expiation; (4) establishment and public proclamation of religion ; (5) ordination of ministers ; (6) appointment of Reporters and provision for public administration of justice ; (7) religious toleration ; (8) the King's abandonment of frivolous pursuits ; (9) condemnation of vain festivities ; (10) the King's desire that his people should be righteous ; (11) the duty of munificence ; (12) only found in a rock-cut inscription at Junágarh ; (13) names of contemporary sovereigns, Antiochus II., Ptolemaios Philadelphus, and Antigonus Gonatas, B.C. 280,—40 or thereabouts ; (14) conclusion. The Monolith at Dehli farther states that the King caused wells to be dug and trees planted, beside the public roads. These or similar cuttings have been found from Yusafza to Gárjám."—*Itihás Timir Nasak*, by Rájá Siva Prasád, C. S. I., Part III.

APPENDIX D.

DEATH OF TOGHLAK SHÁH.

In the travels of Ibn Batuta is the following circumstantial narrative, taken from the lips of an eye-witness :—

"There was then at Dehli a saint, Nizám-ud-din Badáuni. Mahammad, the Sultán's son, often visited him, to pay him respect in the eyes of his followers, and to implore his prayers. The Shaikh was subject to ecstatic fits, in which he lost all control of himself. The Sultán's son directed his servants to let him know when the Shaikh was in one of these fits: When he was seized with a fit the prince was informed, and he went to him. As soon as the Shaikh saw him, he exclaimed, 'We give him the throne.' Afterwards he died while the Sultán was absent, and the Sultán's son, Mahammad, bore his bier upon his shoulder. The father heard of this; he suspected his son, and threatened him. Other actions had already aroused suspicions in Toghlak against his son. He was annoyed to see him buy a great number of slaves, and make magnificent presents to secure friends. Now his anger against him increased. The Sultán was informed that the astrologers had predicted that he would never enter again the city of Dehli on returning from his expedition. He replied by threats against them.

"When he came near to his capital, on his return from the expedition, he ordered his son to build for him a *Palace*, or, as these people call it, a Khusk, near a river, which runs by a place called Afghánpur. Mahammad built it in the course of three days, making it chiefly of wood. It was elevated above the ground and rested on pillars of wood, Mahammad planned it scientifically, and Malik Zádá was charged to see the plans carried out. This man was afterwards known by the title of Khwájá-i-Jahán. His real name was Áhmad, son of Ayás. He was then Inspector of buildings, but he afterwards became chief Wazir of Sultán Mahammad. The object which these two persons kept in view in building the Khusk was this,—that it should fall down with a crash when the elephants touched it in a certain part. The Sultán stopped at this building and feasted the people, who afterwards dispersed. His son asked permission to parade the elephants before him fully accoutred. The Sultán consented.

"Shaikh Rukkindin told me that he was then near the Sultán, and that the Sultán's favourite son was with them. Thereupon Mahammad came and said to the Shaikh, Master, it is now the time for afternoon-prayer, go down and pray. I went down, said the Shaikh, and they brought the elephants up on one side, as the prince and his confidant had arranged. When the animals passed along that side, the building fell down upon the Sultán and his son. I heard the noise, continued the Shaikh, and I returned without having said my prayer. I saw that the building had fallen. The Sultán's son, Mahammad, ordered pick-axes and shovels to be brought to dig and seek for his father, but he made signs for them not to hurry, and the tools were not brought till after sunset. Then they began to dig, and they found the Sultán, who had bent over his son to save him from death. Some assert that Toghlak was taken out dead; others, on the contrary, maintain that he was alive, and that an end was made of him. He was carried away at night to the tomb which he had himself built near the city called after him Toghlakábád, and there he was interred.

"It was to the skilful management of the Wazir Khwájá-i-Jahán, in constructing the edifice which fell upon Toghlak, that he owed the position he held with Sultán Mahammad, and the partiality which the latter had for him. No one, whether Wazir or otherwise, enjoyed anything like the consideration in which he was held by the Sultán, and never attained the high position which he possessed near him."—*From Elliot's History of India by Dowson, Vol. III.*

INDEX.

Calcutta, October 1888.

THACKER, SPINK AND CO.'S
PUBLICATIONS.

Echoes from Old Calcutta: being chiefly Reminiscences of the days of Warren Hastings, Francis, and Impey. By H. E. BUSTEED. Second Edition, enlarged and illustrated. Post 8vo. Rs. 6.

"The book will be read by all interested in India."—*Army and Navy Magazine.*

"Dr. Busteed's valuable and entertaining "Echoes from Old Calcutta" has arrived at a Second Edition, revised, enlarged and illustrated with portraits and other plates rare or quaint. It is a pleasure to reiterate the warm commendation of this instructive and lively volume which its appearance called forth some years since."—*Saturday Review.*

"A series of illustrations which are highly entertaining and instructive of the life and manners of Anglo-Indian Society a hundred years ago . . . His style is always bright and pleasing, and the reader may be assured that open the book where he may, he is certain to happen upon something of a quaint character or of a deeper historical interest filling in the neglected background of history . . . . The book from first to last has not a dull page in it, and it is a work of the kind of which the value will increase with years."—*The Englishman.*

Indian Lyrics. By W. TREGO WEBB, M.A., Professor of English Literature, Presidency College. Fcap. 8vo. Cloth. Rs. 4.

"Vivacious and clever . . . He presents the various sorts and conditions of humanity that comprise the round of life in Bengal in a series of vivid vignettes. . . . . He writes with scholarly directness and finish."—*Saturday Review.*

"A volume of poems of more than ordinary interest and undoubted ability."—*Oxford and Cambridge Undergraduates' Journal.*

"Full of pathos, fun, and wisdom."—*Literary Churchman.*

"This volume is one of the best of its kind that has been published in this country."—*Madras Mail.*

"We are thankful for the literary treat which the perusal of this neat little volume has afforded us."—*Indian Mirror.*

THACKER, SPINK AND CO., CALCUTTA.

Departmental Ditties and other Verses. By RUDYARD KIPLING. Third Edition. With additional Verses. Cloth. Rs. 2.

"This tiny volume will not be undeserving of a place on the bookshelf that holds 'Twenty-one Days in India.' Its contents, indeed, are not unlike the sort of verse we might have expected from poor 'Ali Baba' if he had been spared to give it us. Mr. Kipling resembles him in lightness of touch, quaintness of fancy, and unexpected humour."—*Pioneer.*

"They will suffer little by comparison with the best work of Praed or Locker. Departmental Ditties proper are followed by an anthology of 'other verses,' possessing a variety and a charm which it would be difficult to praise too highly. . . ."—*Englishman.*

"The verses are all written in a light style, which is very attractive, and no one with the slightest appreciation of humour will fail to indulge in many a hearty laugh before turning over the last page."—*Times of India.*

"In this new booklet there are apparent the facility and ingenuity of rhyme, the concise and artly expression, and the light and graceful treatment of his subjects by which Mr. Kipling has already won wide repute as a skilful writer of Indian *Vers de société.* Good-humoured as Mr. Kipling's satire usually is, he can write with scathing force when in a serious mood."

"They are full of humour and spirit, and, brief as they are, have the genuine ring, and display a poetical faculty of a high order. The little publication has already made its mark as among the best of its kind."—*Sind Gazette.*

"He has attacked the public departments of this country, dealing with them in a spirit of genial fun which reminds one of Bon Gaultier and Aliph Cheem combined. . . ."—*Advocate of India.*

"Mr. Kipling's rhymes are rhymes to some purpose. He calls them Departmental Ditties; but they are in reality social sketches of Indian officialism from a single view point that of the satirist, though the satire is of the mildest and most delightful sort."—*Indian Planter's' Gazette.*

Poppied Sleep: A Christmas Story of an Up-country Station. By MRS. H. A. FLETCHER, Author of "Here's Rue for You." Crown 8vo. Sewed. Re. 1-8.

"Here's Rue for You." Novelettes, English and Anglo-Indian. By MRS. H. A. FLETCHER. Crown 8vo. Sewed. Rs. 2.

CONTENTS:—A Summer Madness—Whom the Gods love—Nemesis—A Gathered Rose—At Sea a P and O Story—Esther: an Episode.

Indian-English and Indian Character. By ELLIS UNDERWOOD. Fcap. 8vo. As. 12.

Mookerjee. A Memoir of the late Justice Onoocool Chunder Mookerjee. By M. MOOKERJEE. Third Edition 12mo. Re. 1.

"The reader is earnestly advised to procure the life of this gentleman, written by his nephew, and read it."—*The Tribes on my Frontier.*

Plain Tales from the Hills. By RUDYARD KIPLING, Author of "Departmental Ditties and other Verses." Crown 8vo. Rs. 4.

"Rattling stories of flirtation and sport . . . . Funny stories of practical jokes and sells . . . . Sad little stories of deeper things told with an affectation of solemnity but rather more throat-lumping for that."—*Sunday Times.*

"Mr. Kipling possesses the art of telling a story—"Plain Tales from the Hills" sparkle with fun; they are full of life, merriment and humour, as a rule mirth-provoking. There is at times a pathetic strain, but this soon passes, and laughter, as the Yankees say side-splitting laughter, is the order of the day. There are spits at persons of note, sly allusions to the mysterious ways of Officials in high places and covert attacks on the peculiarities of a great Government. The mirror of satire reflects all and every thing, nothing escapes, and the result is one of the most sparkling, witty and droll collection of tales which could be well conceived."—*Allen's Indian Mail.*

"There is a sustained power of description, knowledge of men and women and terse epigrammatic wit which would suffice to build up half-a-hundred works of fiction. We must be careful to say that while the military flavour of the work is its best characteristic, the Indian civilian, the tea-planter, and the natives high as well as low, in their language, habits, idioms *argot and general* idiosyncracies are sketched in a broad yet crisp artistic fashion."—*The Broad Arrow.*

"Mr. Kipling knows and appreciate the English in India, and is a born story-teller and a man of humour into the bargain. He is also singularly versatile and equally at home in humour and pathos; while neither quality is ever quite absent from his little stories . . . it would be hard to find better reading."—*Saturday Review.*

Son Gruel; or, What he met in the Mofussil (after two Noble Lords). Cantos I and II. Fcap. 8vo. Re. 1 each.

Light and Shade. By HERBERT SHERRING. A collection of Tales and Poems.

The Captain's Daughter: a Novel by A. C. POOSHKIN. Literally translated from the Russian by STUART H. GODFREY, Captain, Bom. S. C. Cr. 8vo.

India in 1983. A Reprint of this celebrated Pamphlet. Fcap. 8vo. Re. 1.

Leviora: being the Rhymes of a Successful Competitor. By the late T. F. BIGNOLD, ESQ., Bengal Civil Service. 8vo. Rs. 7-8.

Cæsar de Souza : EARL OF WAKEFIELD. By the Author of "India in 1983." Crown 8vo. Cloth Rs. 2-8.

The Tribes on My Frontier : An Indian Naturalist's Foreign Policy. By EHA. With 50 Illustrations by F. C. MACRAE. In Imperial 16mo. Uniform with "Lays of Ind." Third Edition. Rs. 6.

This remarkably clever work most graphically and humourously describes the surroundings of a country bungalow. The twenty chapters embrace a year's experiences, and provide endless sources of amusement and suggestion. The numerous able illustrations add very greatly to the interest of the volume, which will find a place on every table.

"We have only to thank our Anglo-Indian naturalist for the delightful book which he has sent home to his countrymen in Britain. May he live to give us another such."—*Chambers' Journal.*

"A most charming series of sprightly and entertaining essays on what may be termed the fauna of the Indian bungalow. . . . . We have no doubt that this amusing book will find its way into every Anglo-Indian's Library."—*Allen's Indian Mail.*

"This is a delightful book, irresistibly funny in description and illustration, but full of genuine science too. . . . . . There is not a dull or uninstructive page in the whole book."—*Knowledge.*

"It is a pleasantly-written book about the insects and other torments of India which make Anglo-Indian life unpleasant, and which can be read with pleasure even by those beyond the reach of the tormenting things Eha describes."—*Graphic.*

Lays of Ind. By ALIPH CHEEM. Comic, Satirical, and Descriptive Poems illustrative of Anglo-Indian Life. Eighth Edition. Enlarged. With 70 Illustrations. Cloth elegant, gilt edges. Rs. 7-8.

"There is no mistaking the humour, and at times, indeed, the fun is both 'fast and furious.' One can readily imagine the merriment created round the camp fire by the recitation of 'The Two Thumpers,' which is irresistibly droll."—*Liverpool Mercury.*

"The 'Lays' are not only Anglo-Indian in origin, but out-and-out Anglo-Indian in subject and colour. To one who knows something of life at an Indian 'station' they will be especially amusing. Their exuberant fun at the same time may well attract the attention of the ill-defined individual known as the 'general reader.'"—*Scotsman.*

"The verses are characterised by high animal spirits, great cleverness, and most excellent fooling."—*World.*

Modern Hinduism: being an Account of the Religion and Life of the Hindus in Northern India. By W. J. WILKINS, of the London Missionary Society, Author of "Hindu Mythology, Vedic and Puranic." Demy 8vo. Rs. 8.

INTRODUCTION.

I.—EARLY LIFE.
1. Birth and its Ceremonies.
2. The Hindu Home.
3. The Guru and Initiation into Hinduism.

II.—HINDU SECTS.
1. General Changes of Hinduism.
2. General Remarks on the Hindu Sects.
3. Vedantism or Orthodox Hinduism.
4. Sects existing in the 14th Cent. A.D.
5. The Vishnava Sects.
6. The Saivite Sects.
7. The Saktas, &c.
8. Miscellaneous Sects.
9. The Modern Deistic Sects.

III.—CASTE.
1. General Remarks on Caste.
2. Caste Distinctions as taught in the Scriptures.
3. History of the Growth of the Caste system.
4. Struggles for Supremacy amongst the Castes.
5. Caste as it exists at the present time.
6. Proportion of People included in the chief Castes.
7. Kulinism.

IV.—WORSHIP.
1. Private Worship.
2. Temple Worship.
3. Religious Festivals.
4. Pilgrimages: Benares.
5. Ditto. Káli Ghât. Ganga Sagar, Gaya.
6. Ditto. Puri.
7. Ditto. Bhuvaenshwara.
8. Worship. How sustained and objects sought by it.
9. Religious ideas common to all Sects expressed in worship.

V.—WOMAN.
1. Position of Woman as taught in the Hindu Scriptures.
2. Present position. Marriage Ceremonies, &c.
3. Widows.
4. Sati.

VI.—MORALS.
1. The Hindus generally.
2. The Criminal Classes.

VII.—DEATH, SHRADH AND FUTURE JUDGMENT.
1. Death and its Ceremonies.
2. The Shradha or Religious Ceremonies on behalf of the departed.
3. Judgment after death; Reward and Punishments.

"He writes in a liberal and comprehensive spirit."—*Saturday Review.*

"Elaborately treated from various points of view."—*Scottish Leader.*

"A volume which is at once a voluminous disquisition upon the Hindu religion, and a most interesting narrative of Hindu life, the habits and customs of the Hindu community and a national Hindu historiette, written with all the verve of the accomplished littérateur, added to the picturesque word-painting and life-like delineations of a veteran novelist."—*Express, Lucknow.*

"A solid addition to our literature."—*Westminster Review.*

"A valuable contribution to knowledge."—*Scotsman.*

"A valuable contribution to the study of a very difficult subject."—*Madras Mail.*

Daily Life in India. By the Rev. W. J. WILKINS. Illustrated. Crown 8vo. Cloth. Rs. 3-12.

CONTENTS:—Calcutta—Calcutta, the Oxford of India—The People: Europeans in India—The People Generally—A Talk about Insects, Reptiles, &c.—A Chapter about the Gods—Hindu Temples—Holy Places and Pilgrims—Religious Festivals—Gurus, or Religious Teachers, and their Disciples—Hindu Saint—Burning Ghâts and Treatment of the Dying—Bazaar Preaching—Life on the River—Life in Tent—All about Tigers—School Work—Work amongst the Hindu Girls and Women—Bengali Christians—India's Need.

Hindu Mythology, Vedic and Puranic. By W. J. WILKINS, of the London Missionary Society, Calcutta. Profusely illustrated. Imperial 16mo. Cloth gilt elegant. Rs. 7.

"His aim has been to give a faithful account of the Hindu deities such as an intelligent native would himself give, and he has endeavoured, in order to achieve his purpose, to keep his mind free from prejudice or theological bias. The author has attempted a work of no little ambition and has succeeded in his attempt, the volume being one of great interest and usefulness."—*Home News.*

"Mr. Wilkins has done his work well, with an honest desire to state facts apart from all theological prepossession, and his volume is likely to be a useful book of reference."—*Guardian.*

"In Mr. Wilkins's book we have an illustrated manual, the study of which will lay a solid foundation for more advanced knowledge, while it will furnish those who may have the desire without having the time or opportunity to go further into the subject, with a really extensive stock of accurate information."—*Indian Daily News.*

The Hindoos as they are; a Description of the Manners, Customs, and Inner Life of Hindoo Society, Bengal. By SHIB CHUNDER BOSE. Second Edition. Revised. Crown 8vo. Cloth. Rs. 5.

Landholding, and the Relation of Landlord and Tenant in Various Countries of the World. By C. D. FIELD, M.A., LL.D. Second Edition. 8vo. Cloth. Rs. 16.

N.B.—This Edition contains "The Bengal Tenancy Act," 1885, with Notes and Observations: and an Index to the whole of the Law of Landlord and Tenant in Bengal.

"We may take it that, as regards Indian laws and customs, Mr. Field shows himself to be at once an able and skilled authority. In order, however, to render his work more complete, he has compiled chiefly from Blue-books and similar public sources, a mass of information having reference to the land-laws of most European countries, of the United States of America, and our Australasian Colonies."—*The Field.*

"Mr. Justice Field has treated his subject with judicial impartiality, and his style of writing is powerful and perspicuous."—*Notes and Queries.*

The Life of H. M. Queen Victoria, Empress of India. By JOHN J. POOL, Editor, *Indian Missionary*. With an Original Portrait from a Wax Medallion by Signor C. Moscatti. Crown 8vo. Paper, Re. 1. Cloth, Re. 1-4.

A Tea Planter's Life in Assam. By GEORGE M. BARKER. With Seventy-five Illustrations by the Author. Crown 8vo. Rs. 5-8.

"Mr. Barker has supplied us with a very good and readable description, accompanied by numerous illustrations drawn by himself. What may be called the business parts of the book are of most value."—*Contemporary Review.*

"Cheery, well-written little book."—*Graphic.*

"A very interesting and amusing book, artistically illustrated from sketches drawn by the Author."—*Mark Lane Express.*

Ancient India as described by Ptolemy. With Introduction, Commentary, Map of India. By J. W. MCCRINDLE, M.A. 8vo. Cloth, lettered. Rs. 4-4.

Ancient India as described by Megasthenes and Arrian. With Introduction, Notes, and a Map of Ancient India. By J. W. MCCRINDLE, M.A. 8vo. Rs. 2-8.

The Commerce and Navigation of the Erythræan Sea; Periplus Maris Erythræi and of Arrian's Account of the Voyage of Nearkhos. With Introduction, Commentary, Notes, and Index. By J. W. MCCRINDLE, M.A. 8vo. Rs. 3.

Ancient India as described by Ktesias the Knidian; being a Translation of the Abridgment of his 'Indika,' by Photios. With Introduction, Notes, and Index. By J. W. MCCRINDLE, M.A. 8vo. Rs. 3.

Book of Indian Eras, with Tables for calculating Indian Dates. By ALEXANDER CUNNINGHAM, C.S.I., C.I.E., Major-General, Royal Engineers. Royal 8vo. Cloth. Rs. 12.

Our Administration of India: being a complete Account of the Revenue and Collectorate Administration in all Departments, with special reference to the Work and Duties of a District Officer in Bengal. By H. A. D. PHILLIPS. Rs. 4-4.

In eleven chapters Mr. Phillips gives a complete epitome of the civil, in distinction from the criminal, duties of an Indian Collector."—*London Quarterly Review.*

It contains much information in a convenient form for English readers, who wish to study the working of our system in the country districts of India."—*Westminster Review.*

"A very handy and useful book of information upon a very momentous subject, about which Englishmen know very little."—*Pall Mall Gazette.*

THACKER, SPINK AND CO., CALCUTTA.

The Trial of Maharaja Nanda Kumar: A Narrative of a Judicial Murder. By H. BEVERIDGE, Bengal Civil Service. Demy 8vo. Rs. 5.

Tales from Indian History: being the Annals of India retold in Narratives. By J. TALBOYS WHEELER. Crown 8vo. Cloth, gilt. Rs. 3-4.

"No one can read a volume such as this without being deeply interested."—*Scotsman.*

"The history of our great dependency made extremely attractive reading. Altogether this is a work of rare merit."—*Broad Arrow.*

"In going through an interesting book, the reader will be furnished with a good general notion of Indian history, and learn besides something about Indian modes of life."—*Queen.*

"Will absorb the attention of all who delight in thrilling records of adventure and daring. It is no mere compilation, but an earnest and brightly written book."—*Daily Chronicle.*

Kashgaria (Eastern or Chinese Turkestan), Historical, Geographical, Military, and Industrial. By Col. KUROPATKIN, Russian Army. Translated by Major GOWAN, H. M.'s Indian Army. 8vo. Rs. 6-8

Mandalay to Momien: a Narrative of the Two Expeditions to Western China of 1868 and 1875, under Cols. E. B. Sladen and H. Browne. Three Maps, numerous Views and Woodcuts. By JOHN ANDERSON, M. D. Thick demy 8vo. Cloth. Rs. 5.

British Burma and its People: being Sketches of Native Manners, Customs, and Religion. By Capt. C. J. F. S. FORBES. 8vo. Cloth. Rs. 4-8.

Myam-Ma: **the Home of the Burman.** By TSAYA (Rev. H. POWELL). Crown 8vo. Rs. 2.

A Critical Exposition of the Popular "Jihad," showing that all the Wars of Mahammad were defensive, and that Aggressive War or compulsory Conversion is not allowed in the Koran, &c. By Moulavi CHERAGH ALI, Author of "Reforms under Moslem Rule," "Hyderabad under Sir Salar Jung." 8vo. Rs. 6.

Hints for the Management and Medical Treatment of Children in India. By EDWARD A. BIRCH, M.D., Surgeon-Major, Bengal Establishment. Second Edition, Revised. Being the Eighth Edition of "Goodeve's Hints for the Management of Children in India." Crown 8vo. Rs. 7.

Dr. Goodeve.—"I have no hesitation in saying that the present edition is for many reasons superior to its predecessors. It is written very carefully, and with much knowledge and experience on the author's part, whilst it possesses the great advantage of bringing up the subject to the present level of Medical Science."

The Medical Times and Gazette, in an article upon this work and Moore's "Family Medicine for India," says:—"The two works before us are in themselves probably about the best examples of medical works written for non-professional readers. The style of each is simple, and as free as possible from technical expressions. The modes of treatment recommended are generally those most likely to yield good results in the hands of laymen; and throughout each volume the important fact is kept constantly before the mind of the reader, that the volume he is using is but a poor substitute for personal professional advice, for which it must be discarded whenever there is the opportunity."

Firminger's Manual of Gardening for India. A New Edition, thoroughly revised and re-written. With many Illustrations. By J. H. JACKSON.

Queries at a Mess Table. What shall we Eat? What shall we Drink? By Surgeon-Major JOSHUA DUKE. Fcap. 8vo. Cloth, gilt. Rs. 2-4.

Banting in India. With some Remarks on Diet and Things in general. By Surgeon-Major JOSHUA DUKE. Third Edition. Cloth. Re. 1-8.

English Etiquette for Indian Gentlemen. By W. TREGO WEBB, Bengal Educational Department. Fcap. 8vo. Cloth. Re. 1-4. Paper. Re. 1.

The book comprises chapters on General Conduct, Calls, Dining-out, Levees, Balls, Garden-parties, Railway-travelling, &c.

It also contains a chapter on Letter-writing, proper Modes of address, &c., together with hints on How to draw up Applications for Appointments, with examples.

The Indian Cookery Book. A Practical Handbook to the Kitchen in India, adapted to the Three Presidencies. Containing Original and Approved Recipes in every department of Indian Cookery; Recipes for Summer Beverages and Home-made Liqueurs; Medicinal and other Recipes; together with a variety of things worth knowing. By a Thirty-five Years' Resident. Rs. 3.

Weterinary Notes for Horse-Owners: An Everyday Horse Book. By Captain M. HORACE HAYES.

"The work is written in a clear and practical way."—*Saturday Review.*

"Of the many popular veterinary books which have come under our otice, this is certainly one of the most scientific and reliable. . . . . The escription of symptoms and the directions for the application of remedies re given in perfectly plain terms, which the tyro will find no difficulty in omprehending."—*The Field.*

"Simplicity is one of the most commendable features in the book."—*llustrated Sporting and Dramatic News.*

"We heartily welcome the second edition of this exceedingly useful ook."—*The Sporting Life.*

"Captain Hayes, in the new edition of 'Veterinary Notes,' has added onsiderably to its value, and rendered the book more useful to those non-rofessional people who may be inclined or compelled to treat their own orses when sick or injured."—*Veterinary Journal.*

"We do not think that horse-owners in general are likely to find a more eliable and useful book for guidance in an emergency."—*The Field.*

raining and Horse Management in India. By Captain M. HORACE HAYES, Author of "Veterinary Notes for Horse-Owners," "Riding," &c. Third Edition. Crown 8vo. Rs. 5.

"No better guide could be placed in the hands of either amateur horse-ian or veterinary surgeon."—*The Veterinary Journal.*

"A useful guide in regard to horses anywhere. . . . . . Concise, ·actical, and portable."—*Saturday Review.*

adian Horse Notes: an Epitome of useful Information arranged for ready reference on Emergencies, and specially adapted for Officers and Mofussil Residents. All Technical Terms explained and Simplest Remedies selected. By Major C——. Author of "Indian Notes about Dogs." Second Edition, Revised and considerably Enlarged. Fcap. 8vo. Cloth. Rs. 2.

ıdian Notes about Dogs: their Diseases and Treatment. By Major C——. Third Edition, Revised. Fcap. 8vo. Cloth. Re. 1-8.

eonee: or, Camp Life on the Satpura Range. A Tale of Indian Adventure. By R. A. STERNDALE, Author of "Mammalia of India," "Denizens of the Jungles." Illustrated by the Author. With a Map and an Appendix containing a brief Topographical and Historical Account of the District of Seonee in the Central Provinces of India. Cr. 8vo. Cloth. Rs. 6.

Large Game Shooting in Thibet, the Himalayas, and Northern India. By Colonel ALEXANDER A. KINLOCH. Containing Descriptions of the Country and of the various Animals to be found; together with Extracts from a Journal of several years' standing. With Thirty Illustrations and Map. Demy 4to., elegantly bound. Rs. 25.

"An attractive volume, full of sporting adventures in the valleys and forest hills extending along the foot of the Himalayas. Its pages are also interesting for the graphic description they give of the beasts of the field, the cunning instinct which they show in guarding their safety, the places which they choose for their lair, and the way in which they show their anger when at bay. Colonel Kinloch writes on all these subjects in a genuine and straightforward style, aiming at giving a complete description of the habits and movements of the game."—*British Mail.*

"The splendidly illustrated record of sport. The photo-gravures, especially the heads of the various antelopes, are lifelike; and the letterpress is very pleasant reading."—*Graphic.*

Denizens of the Jungle; a Series of Sketches of Wild Animals illustrating their form and natural attitude. With Letterpress Description of each Plate. By R. A. STERNDALE, F.R.G.S., F.Z.S., Author of "Natural History of the Mammalia of India," "Seonee," &c. Oblong folio. Rs. 10.

I.—Denizens of the Jungles. Aborigines—Deer—Monkeys.
II.—"On the Watch." Tiger.
III.—"Not so Fast Asleep as he Looks."—Panther—Monkeys.
IV.—"Waiting for Father." Black Bears of the Plains.
V.—"Rival Monarchs." Tiger and Elephant.
VI.—"Hors de Combat." Indian Wild Boar and Tiger.
VII.—"A Race for Life." Blue Bull and Wild Dogs.
VIII.—"Meaning Mischief." The Gaur—Indian Bison.
IX.—"More than His Match." Buffalo and Rhinoceros.
X.—"A Critical Moment." Spotted Deer and Leopard.
XI.—"Hard Hit." The Sambur.
XII.—"Mountain Monarchs." Marco Polo's Sheep.

Useful Hints to Young Shikaris on the Gun and Rifle. By "THE LITTLE OLD BEAR." Reprinted from the *Asian*. Crown 8vo. Rs. 2-8.

Game, Shore, and Water Birds of India. By Col. A. LE MESSURIER, R.E., with 121 Illustrations. A *vade mecum* for Sportsmen. 8vo. Rs. 10; cash 9.

Soundness and Age of Horses: A Veterinary and Legal Guide to the Examination of Horses for Soundness. By M. HORACE HAYES, M.R.C.V.S. 100 Illustrations. Crown 8vo. Rs. 6.

On Horse Breaking. By Capt. M. H. HAYES. Numerous Illustrations by J. H. OSWALD BROWN. Square. [*In the Press.*

1. Theory of Horse Breaking. 2. Principles of Mounting. 3. Horse Control. 4. Rendering Docile. 5. Giving Good Mouths. 6. Teaching to Jump. 7. Mount for First Time. 8. Breaking for Ladies' Riding. 9. Breaking to Harness. 10. Faults of mouth. 11. Nervousness and Impatience. 12. Jibbing. 13. Jumping Faults. 14. Faults in Harness. 15. Aggressiveness. 16. Riding and Driving Newly-Broken Horse. 17. Stable Vices.

The Points of the Horse. A Familiar Treatise on Equine Conformation. By Capt. M. H. HAYES. Illustrated by J. H. OSWALD BROWN. Describing the points in which the perfection of each class of horses consists; illustrated by very numerous reproductions of Photographs of Living Typical Animals: forming an invaluable guide to owners of horses. [*In the Press.*

Riding: on the Flat and Across Country. A Guide to Practical Horsemanship. By Capt. M. H. HAYES. Illustrated by Sturgess. Second Edition. Revised and Enlarged. Rs. 7-8.

"The book is one that no man who has ever sat in a saddle can fail to read with interest."—*Illustrated Sporting and Dramatic News.*

"An excellent book on riding."—*Truth.*

"Is as practical as Captain Horace Hayes' 'Veterinary Notes' and Guide to Horse Management in India.' Greater praise than this it is impossible to give."—*Graphic.*

"To possess knowledge, and to succeed in imparting it, are two different things; but Captain Hayes is not only a master of his subject, but he knows how to aid others in gaining such a mastery as may be obtained by the study of a book."—*The Standard.*

"We heartily commend it to our readers."—*Sporting Times.*

Riding for Ladies, with Hints on the Stable. A Lady's Horse Book. By Mrs. POWER O'DONOGHUE. With 75 Illustrations, by A. CHANTREY CORBOULD. Elegantly printed and bound. Imperial 16mo., gilt. Rs. 10; cash 9.

I.—Ought Children to Ride?
II.—"For Mothers and Children."
III.—First Hints to a Learner.
IV.—Selecting a Mount.
V.—The Lady's Dress.
VI.—Ditto.
VII.—Bitting.
VIII.—Saddling.
IX.—How to Sit, Walk, Canter, and Trot.
X.—Reins, Voice, and Whip.
XI.—Riding on the Road.
XII.—Paces, Vices, and Faults.
XIII.—A Lesson in Leaping.
XIV.—Managing Refusers.
XV.—Falling.
XVI.—Hunting Outfit Considered.
XVII.—Economy in Riding Dress.
XVIII.—Hacks and Hunters.
XIX.—In the Hunting Field.
XX.—Shoeing.
XXI.—Feeding.
XXII.—Stabling.
XXIII.—Doctoring.
XXIV.—Breeding.
XXV.—"Wrinkles."

ndian Racing Reminiscences. Being Entertaining Narratives and Anecdotes of Men, Horses, and Sport. By Capt. HAYES. Illustrated with 22 Portraits and 20 Engravings. Imperial 16mo. Rs. 6.

"Captain Hayes has done wisely in publishing these lively sketches of life in India. The book is full of racy anecdote."—*Bell's Life.*

"All sportsmen who can appreciate a book on racing, written in a chatty style, and full of anecdote, will like Captain Hayes's latest work."—*Field.*

"It is a safe prediction that this work is certain to have a wide circle of readers."—*Broad Arrow.*

"The book is valuable from the fact that many hints on the treatment of horses are included, and the accuracy and extent of Captain Hayes's veterinary skill and knowledge are well known to experts."—*Illustrated Sporting and Dramatic News.*

"Many a racing anecdote and many a curious character our readers will find in the book, which is very well got up, and embellished with many portraits."—*Baily's Magazine.*

Calcutta Turf Club Rules of Racing, together with the Rules relating to Lotteries, Betting, and Defaulters and the Rules of the Calcutta Turf Club. Authorized Edition. Rs. 2.

Calcutta Racing Calendar. Published fortnightly. Annual Subscription, Rs. 12.

Manual of Agriculture for India. By Lieut. FREDERICK POGSON. Illustrated crown 8vo. Cloth, gilt. Rs. 5; cash 4-8.

Roxburgh's Flora Indica; or, Description of Indian Plants. Reprinted literatim from Cary's Edition. 8vo. Cloth. Rs. 5.

A Natural History of the Mammalia of India, Burmah and Ceylon. By R. A. STERNDALE, F.R.G.S., F.Z.S., &c., Author of "Seonee," "The Denizens of the Jungle." With 170 Illustrations by the Author and Others. In Imperial 16mo. Rs. 10; cash 9.

"It is the very model of what a popular natural history should be."—*Knowledge.*

"The notices of each animal are, as a rule, short, though on some of the larger mammals—the lion, tiger, pard, boar, &c.—ample and interesting details are given, including occasional anecdotes of adventure. The book will, no doubt, be specially useful to the sportsman, and, indeed, has been extended so as to include all territories likely to be reached by the sportsman from India."—*The Times.*

Handbook to the Ferns of India, Ceylon, and the Malay Peninsula. By Colonel R. H. BEDDOME, Author of the "Ferns of British India." Three hundred Illustrations by the Author. Imperial 16mo. Rs. 10 ; cash 9.

"The great amount of care observed in its compilation makes it a most valuable work of reference."—*Garden.*

"It is the first special book of portable size and moderate price which has been devoted to Indian Ferns, and is in every way deserving of the extensive circulation it is sure to obtain."—*Nature.*

The Culture and Manufacture of Indigo, with a Description of a Planter's Life and Resources. By WALTER MACLAGAN REID. Crown 8vo. With nineteen full-page Illustrations. Rs. 5.

"It is proposed in the following Sketches of Indigo Life in Tirhoot and Lower Bengal to give those who have never witnessed the manufacture of Indigo, or seen an Indigo Factory in this country, an idea of how the finished marketable article is produced: together with other phases and incidents of an Indigo Planter's life, such as may be interesting and amusing to friends at home."—*Introduction.*

The Landmarks of Snake-poison Literature; being a Review of the more important Researches into the Nature of Snake-poisons. By VINCENT RICHARDS, F.R.C.S., ED., &c., Civil Medical Officer of Goalundo, Bengal. Rs. 2-8.

The Future of the Date Palm in India. (Phœnix Dactylifera.) By E. BONAVIA, M.D., Brigade-Surgeon, Indian Medical Department. Crown 8vo. Cloth. Rs. 2-8.

Statistics of Hydraulic Works, and Hydrology of England, Canada, Egypt, and India. Collected and reduced by LOWIS D'A. JACKSON, C.E., Author of "Canal and Culvert Tables," "Hydraulic Manual," "Aid to Engineering Solution." In royal 8vo. Rs. 10.

"In this work a successful attempt has been made to collect and arrange in a systematic order facts and data. . . . The order in which the subjects are arranged being river basins: their area in square miles, geology and rainfall, canals and navigation, storage works, irrigation with sewage, analysis of water and of factory effluents, &c. The statistics relating to canals have been compiled with much care. Irrigation with sewage, is a full and complete chapter. The analysis of water will be welcomed as a very useful summary. The hydrology of Canada, Egypt, and India, especially the latter is very carefully tabulated. The latter portion of Mr. Jackson's laborious work will be of considerable value to engineers of the Indian Public Works Departments."—*Building News.*

Malaria; its Cause and Effects. Malaria and the Spleen; Injuries of the Spleen: An Analysis of 39 Cases. By E. G. RUSSELL, M.B., B.S.C. 8vo., cloth. Rs. 8.

A Record of Three years' Work of the National Association for Supplying Female Medical Aid to the Women of India. August 1885 to August 1888. By The COUNTESS OF DUFFERIN. Cr. 8vo. Re. 1.

The National Association for Supplying Female Medical Aid to the Women of India. By H. E. The COUNTESS of DUFFERIN. Reprinted from the "Asiatic Quarterly Review," by Permission. As. 8.

The Bengal Medical Service, April, 1885. Compiled by G. F. A. HARRIS, Surgeon, Bengal Medical Service. Royal 8vo. Rs. 2.

Ague; or, Intermittent Fever. By M. D. O'CONNELL, M.D. 8vo. Sewed. Rs. 2.

Life: An Explanation of it. By W. SEDGWICK, Major, R.E. Crown 8vo. Cloth. Rs. 2.

Map of the Civil Divisions of India. Including Governments, Divisions and Districts, Political Agencies, and Native States; also the Cities and Towns with 10,000 Inhabitants and upwards. Coloured, 20 in. × 36 in. Folded, Re. 1. On linen, Rs. 2.

Calcutta to Liverpool by China, Japan, and America in 1877. By Lieut.-General Sir HENRY NORMAN. Second Edition. Fcap. 8vo. Cloth. Rs. 2-8.

Guide to Masuri, Landaur, Dehra Dun, and the Hills North of Dehra; including Routes to the Snows and other places of note; with Chapter on Garhwal (Tehri), Hardwar, Rurki, and Chakrata. By JOHN NORTHAM. Rs. 2-8.

A Handbook for Visitors to Agra and its Neighbourhood. By H. G. KEENE, C.S. Fifth Edition, Revised. Maps, Plans, &c. Fcap. 8vo. Cloth. Rs. 2-8.

A Handbook for Visitors to Delhi and its Neighbourhood. By H. G. KEENE, C.S. Third Edition. Maps. Fcap. 8vo. Cloth. Rs. 2-8.

Ince's Kashmir Hand-book. Revised and Re-written. By Surgeon-Major JOSHUA DUKE. With 4 Maps. Fcap. 8vo. Cloth. Rs. 6.

Hills beyond Simla. Three Months' Tour from Simla, through Bussahir, Kunowar, and Spiti, to Lahoul. ("In the Footsteps of the Few.") By MRS. J. C. MURRAY-AYNSLEY. Crown 8vo. Cloth. Rs. 3.

From the City of Palaces to Ultima Thule. With a Map of Iceland, Icelandic Vocabulary, Money Tables, etc. By H. K. GORDON. Crown 8vo. Sewed. Re. 1.

.888.—Thacker's Indian Directory. Official, Legal, Educational, Professional, and Commercial Directories of the whole of India. With a Complete Directory, including the Streets of the Cities of Calcutta, Bombay, Madras, Allahabad, Rangoon, &c.; Almanac and General Information, Holidays, &c.; Stamp Duties, Customs Tariff, Tonnage Schedules; Post Offices in India forming a Gazetteer; Lists of Governors-General and Administrators of India from beginning of British Rules; Orders of the Star of India, Indian Empire, &c.; Warrant of Precedence, Table of Salutes, &c.; An Army List of the Three Presidencies; A Newspaper and Periodical Directory; A Conveyance Directory for the whole of India; Tea, Indigo, Silk, and Coffee Concerns, with Details of Acreage, Management, and Trade Marks; List of Clubs in India; Alphabetical List of Residents; Alphabetical List of the Principal Native Residents. In thick Royal Octavo. Price, Rs. 16, cash; Post-free, 16-12.

Complete List of Indian Tea Gardens, Indigo Concerns, Silk Filatures, Sugar Factories, Cinchona Concerns, and Coffee Estates. With their Capital, Directors, Proprietors, Agents, Managers, Assistants, &c., and their Factory Marks by which the chests may be identified in the market. Rs. 2-8.

ıpplement containing List of CEYLON Tea Gardens with their Acreage. Re. 1.

ıeroes' Indian and English Exchange Tables. New Edition. In this Edition the rate rises by 32nds of a penny, the progression of the numbers is by units; thus, in most instances, saving a line of calculation. Facility of reference and accuracy render it the most perfect work in existence. (1*s.* 4*d.* to 1*s.* 8*d.*) Demy 8vo. Rs. 10.

The Indian Tribute and the Loss by Exchange: An Essay on the Depreciation of Indian Commodities in England; shewing why the growth of the Home-charges has been accompanied by a fall in the English value of Indian Exports; the inevitable effect of this fall on the Gold-price of Silver and the Rate of Exchange; and the utter failure of Bimetallism as a remedy for India's growing burden. By THOMAS INWOOD POLLARD, Author of "Gold and Silver Weighed in the Balance." Crown 8vo. Cloth. Rs. 2-8.

Gold and Silver Weighed in the Balance: A Measure of their Value; and Essay on Wealth and its Distributions during Fluctuations in the value of Gold and Silver; shewing how the unjust and unintended Gains and Losses that have hitherto accompanied Depreciation and Appreciation of the Precious Metals may be for ever prevented. By THOMAS INWOOD POLLARD, Author of "The Indian Tribute and the Loss by Exchange." Crown 8vo. Rs. 2-8.

The Sepoy Officers' Manual. Second Edition. Revised. By Captain E. G. BARROW. Rs. 2-8.

The Indian Articles of War.—Annotated. By Captain H. S. HUDSON, 27th Madras Infantry. Crown 8vo. Rs. 4.

Musketry Instruction in the form of Question and Answer. By Captain L. E. DUMOULIN. Fcap. 8vo. Rs. 2.

Musketry made Easy for Native Officers and Non-Commissioned Officers, Native Army. By Lieutenant R. E. S. TAYLOR, Adjutant, 38th Bengal Infantry. Arranged in Questions and Answers. English and Urdu. 8 annas.

The Reconnoitrer's Guide and Field Book, adapted for India. By Major M. J. KING-HARMAN, B.S.C. Second Edition, Revised and Enlarged. In roan. Rs. 4.

It contains all that is required for the guidance of the Military Reconnoitrer in India: it can be used as an ordinary Pocket Note Book, or as a Field Message Book; the pages are ruled as a Field Book, and in sections, for written description or sketch.

"To officers serving in India this guide will be invaluable."—*Broad Arrow.*

The Invasion and Defence of England. By Captain F. N. MAUDE, R.E. Crown 8vo. Cloth. Re. 1-8.

Letters on Tactics and Organization. By Captain F. N. MAUDE, R.E. (papers reprinted from "*The Pioneer*" and "*Civil and Military Gazette.*") Crown 8vo. Cloth. Rs. 5.

The Student's Manual of Tactics. By Capt. M. HORACE HAYES. Specially written for the use of Candidates preparing for the Militia, Military Competitive Examinations, and for Promotion. Crown 8vo. Rs. 4-4.

Definitions.
I. Composition of an Army.
II. Infantry.
III. Artillery.
IV. Cavalry.
V. Formations: Time and Space.
VI. Outposts.
VII. Screening and Reconnoitring.
VIII. Advanced Guards.
IX. Rear Guards.
X. Marches.
XI. The Attack.
XII. The Defence.
XIII. Villages.
XIV. Woods.
XV. Machine Guns.

"There is no better Manual on Tactics than the one which Captain Hayes has written."—*Naval and Military Gazette.*

"'The Student's Manual of Tactics' is an excellent book. Principles are reasoned out, and details explained in such a way that the student cannot fail to get a good grasp of the subject. Having served in both the artillery and infantry, and being a practical writer, as well as 'a coach,' the author of this Manual had exceptional qualifications for the task he has accomplished."—*Broad Arrow.*

Notes on the Garrison Course of Instruction.—By Major E. LLOYD. With Diagrams. Crown 8vo. Cloth Rs. 2-8.

A Summary of the Drill and Working of the three Arms. By Colonel H. J. HALLOWES. Revised according to Army Orders, April 1888. Cloth. Re. 1.

MAP OF THE CIVIL DIVISIONS OF INDIA,

INCLUDING

GOVERNMENTS, DIVISIONS AND DISTRICTS, POLITICAL AGENCIES AND NATIVE STATES; ALSO THE CITIES AND TOWNS WITH 10,000 INHABITANTS AND UPWARDS.

Elaborately Coloured, 20 inches by 36 inches.

Folded, Re. 1 ; Mounted on cloth and folded, Rs. 2.
Mounted on roller and varnished, Rs. 3.

THACKER, SPINK AND CO., CALCUTTA.

The Principles of Heat: for the F. A. Examination of the Calcutta University; to which are added Solutions of all the Physical Questions set in the papers of 1885. By LEONARD HALL, M.A., late Scholar of St. John's College, Cambridge. Crown 8vo. As. 8.

A Short Indian History. By PRINGLE KENNEDY, M.A. Crown 8vo. Stitched. As 12.

Analysis of Reid's Enquiry into the Human Mind. With Copious Notes. By W. C. FINK. Second Edition. Re. 1-12.

English People (The) and their Language. Translated from the German of Loth by C. H. TAWNEY, M.A., Professor in the Presidency College, Calcutta. Stitched. As. 8.

An Inquiry into the Human Mind on the Principles of Common Sense. By THOMAS REID, D.D. 8vo. Cloth. Re. 1-4.

Tales from Indian History: being the Annals of India retold in Narratives. By J. TALBOYS WHEELER. Crown 8vo. Cloth. School Edition. Re. 1-12.

A Text-book of Indian Botany, Morphological, Physiological, and Systematic. By W. H. GREGG, B.M.S., Lecturer on Botany at the Hugli Government College. Profusely illustrated. Crown 8vo. Rs. 5.

A Moral Reading Book from English and Oriental Sources. By ROPER LETHBRIDGE, C.I.E., M.A. Crown 8vo. Cloth. As. 14.

A Primer Catechism of Sanitation for Indian Schools. Founded on Dr. Cunningham's Sanitary Primer. By L. A. STAPLEY. As. 4.

Notes on Mill's Examination of Hamilton's Philosophy. The Relativity and the Unconditioned, being some remarks on John Stuart Mill's Examination of Sir William Hamilton's Philosophy. By THOMAS EDWARDS, F.E.I.S. Fcap. Sewed. Re. 1.

A Short History of the English Language. By THOMAS EDWARDS, ESQ., F.E.I.S. 18mo. Re. 1-4.

THE INDIAN MEDICAL GAZETTE. A Record of Medicine, Surgery and Public Health, and of General Medical Intelligence, Indian and Europèan. Edited by K. McLeod, M.D.

Published Monthly. Subscription Rs.* 18 *per Annum, including Postage.

The Indian Medical Gazette was established nineteen years ago, and has earned for itself a world-wide reputation by its solid contributions to Tropical Medicine and Surgery. It is the **Sole** representative medium for recording the work and experience of the Medical Profession in India; and its very numerous **Exchanges** with all the leading Medical Journals in Great Britain and America enable it not only to diffuse this information broadcast throughout the world, but also to call for its Indian readers, from an unusual variety of sources, all information which has any practical bearing on medical works in India.

The Indian Medical Gazette is indispensable to every Member of the Medical Profession in India who wishes to keep himself abreast of medical progress, for it brings together and fixes the very special knowledge which is only to be obtained by long experience and close observation in India. In the way it constitutes itself a record of permanent value for reference, and a journal which ought to be in the library of every medical man in India or connected with that country.

The *Gazette* covers altogether different ground from *The Lancet* and *British Medical Journal*, and in no way competes with these for general information, although it chronicles the most important items of European Medical Intelligence. The whole aim of the *Gazette* is to make itself of special use and value to Medical Officers in India, and to assist and support them in the performance of their difficult duties.

It is specially devoted to the best interests of **The Medical Services**, and its long-established reputation and authority enable it to command serious attention in the advocacy of any desirable reform or substantial grievance.

The **Contributors** to *The Indian Medical Gazette* comprise the most eminent and representative men in the profession.

THACKER, SPINK AND CO., CALCUTTA.

INDIAN LAW BOOKS.

Agnew and Henderson.—The Code of Criminal Procedure (Act X of 1882), together with Rulings, Circular Orders, Notifications, &c., of all the High Courts in India, and Notifications and Orders of the Government of India and the Local Governments. Edited, with Copious Notes and Full Index, By W. F. AGNEW, ESQ., Barrister-at-Law, Author of "A Treatise on the Law of Trusts in India;" and GILBERT S. HENDERSON, ESQ., M.A., Barrister-at-Law, Author of "A Treatise on the Law of Testamentary and Intestate Succession in India." Second Edition. Royal 8vo. Cloth. Rs. 18. [1886.

Beverley.—The Land Acquisition Acts (Act X of 1870 and XVIII of 1885.) With Introduction and Notes. The whole forming complete Manual of Law and Practice on the subject of Compensation for Lands taken for Public Purposes. Applicable to all India. By H. BEVERLEY, ESQ., M.A., B.C.S. Second Edition. 8vo. Cloth. Rs. 6.

Bonnerjee.—The Hindu Wills Act (Act XXI of 1870). With the Sections of the Indian Succession Act (Act X of 1865) made applicable to the Wills of Hindus, Jainas, Sikhs, and Buddhists, printed *in extenso* and in consecutive order. Edited by W. C. BONNERJEE, ESQ. 8vo. Cloth. Rs. 6.

Broughton.—The Code of Civil Procedure; being Act X of 1877. With Notes and Appendix. By the Hon'ble L. P. DELVES BROUGHTON, assisted by Messrs. W. F. AGNEW and G. S. HENDERSON. Royal 8vo. Cloth. Reduced to Rs. 7.

Carnegy.—Kachahri Technicalities: a Glossary of Terms, Rural, Official and General, in daily use in the Courts of Law, and in Illustration of the Tenures, Customs, Arts, and Manufactures of Hindustan. By P. CARNEGY, ESQ. Second Edition. 8vo. Cloth. Rs. 9.

THACKER, SPINK AND CO., CALCUTTA.

Chalmers.—The Negotiable Instruments Act, 1881; being an Act to define and amend the Law relating to Promissory Notes, Bills-of-Exchange, and Cheques. Edited by M. D. CHALMERS, ESQ., M.A., Barrister-at-Law, Author of "A Digest of the Law of Bills-of-Exchange," &c.; and Editor of Wilson's "Judicature Acts." 8vo. Cloth. Rs. 7-8.

Civil Procedure Code; being Act XIV of 1882. With Table of Contents and Index. Royal 8vo. Cloth. Rs. 4-8; Interleaved, Rs. 5-8.

Collett.—The Law of Specific Relief in India; being a Commentary on Act I of 1877. By CHARLES COLLETT, ESQ., late of the Madras Civil Service, of Lincoln's Inn, Barrister-at-Law, and formerly a Judge of the High Court at Madras. Demy 8vo. Rs. 10.

Collier.—The Bengal Local Self-Government Act (B. C. Act III of 1885), and the General Rules framed thereunder. With Notes, Hints regarding Procedure, and References to Leading Cases; an Appendix, containing the principal Acts referred to, etc., etc. By F. R. STANLEY COLLIER, B.C.S. Second Edition. Crown 8vo. Rs. 5.

THE BENGAL MUNICIPAL MANUAL; being B. C. Act III of 1884. With Notes and an Appendix containing all the Acts and Rules relating to Municipalities. By F. R. STANLEY COLLIER, C. S. Second Edition. Crown 8vo. Cloth. Rs. 5.

Cowell.—Hindu Law; being a Treatise on the Law Administered exclusively to Hindus by the British Courts in India. The Tagore Law Lectures, 1870 and 1871. By HERBERT COWELL, Barrister-at-Law. Royal 8vo. Cloth. Lectures, 1870, Rs. 12. Lectures, 1871, Rs. 8.

THE HISTORY AND CONSTITUTION OF THE COURTS AND LEGISLATIVE AUTHORITIES IN INDIA. Second Edition, Revised. By HERBERT COWELL. 8vo. Cloth. Rs. 6. [1884.

Criminal Procedure Code; being Act X of 1882. With Table of Contents and Index. Royal 8vo. Cloth. Rs. 4; Interleaved, Rs. 5.

Cunningham and Shephard.—The Indian Contract Act (No. IX of 1872); together with an Introduction and Explanatory Notes, Table of Contents, Appendix, and Index. By the Hon'ble H. S. CUNNINGHAM, M.A., Barrister-at-Law, one of the Judges of Her Majesty's High Court at Calcutta; and H. H. SHEPHARD, ESQ., M.A., Barrister-at-Law, Madras High Court. Fifth Edition. Demy 8vo. Rs. 15.

Currie.—The Indian Law Examination Manual. By FENDALL CURRIE, ESQ., of Lincoln's Inn, Barrister-at-Law. Third Edition. Demy 8vo. Rs. 5.

CONTENTS:—Introduction—Hindoo Law—Mahomedan Law—Indian Penal Code—Code of Civil Procedure—Evidence Act—Limitation Act—Succession Act—Contract Act—Registration Act—Stamp Acts and Court-Fees—Mortgage—Code of Criminal Procedure—The Easement Act—The Trust Act—The Transfer of Property Act—The Negotiable Instruments Act.

Donogh.—The Stamp Law of British India, as constituted by the Indian Stamp Act (No. I of 1879); Rulings and Circular Orders of the four High Courts; Notifications, Resolutions, Rules, and Orders of the Government of India, and of the various Local Governments up to date; together with Schedules of all the Stamp Duties chargeable on instruments in India from the earliest times. Edited, with Notes and complete Index, by WALTER R. DONOGH, M.A., of the Inner Temple, Barrister-at-Law. Demy 8vo. Cloth, gilt. Rs. 8. [1886.

Field.—THE LAW OF EVIDENCE IN BRITISH INDIA; being a Treatise on the Indian Evidence Act as amended by Act XVIII of 1872. By the Hon'ble C. D. FIELD, M.A., LL.D. Fourth Edition. Thick 8vo. Rs. 18. [1884.

LANDHOLDING and the Relation of Landlord and Tenant in various Countries of the World. By C. D. FIELD, M. A., LL.D., B.C.S., one of the Judges of H. M.'s High Court of Judicature in Bengal. Second Edition. 8vo. Cloth. Rs. 17-12; cash 16. [1885.

INTRODUCTION TO THE REGULATIONS OF THE BENGAL CODE. By C. D. FIELD. Crown 8vo. Rs. 3. [1888.

Finucane and Rampini.—The Bengal Tenancy Act; being Act VIII of 1885. With Notes and Annotations, Judicial Rulings and the Rules framed by the Local Government and the High Court under the Act, for the guidance of Revenue Officers and the Civil Courts. By R. F. RAMPINI, M.A., C.S., Barrister-at-Law, and M. FINUCANE, M.A., C.S.

Forsyth.—Revenue Sale-Law of Lower Bengal, comprising Act XI of 1859; Bengal Act VII of 1868; Bengal Act VII of 1880 (The Public Demands Recovery Act), and the Unrepealed Regulations and the Rules of the Board of Revenue on the subject. With Notes. Edited by WM. E. H. FORSYTH, ESQ. Demy 8vo. Cloth. Rs. 5.

THE PROBATE AND ADMINISTRATION ACT; being Act V of 1881. With Notes. By W. E. H. FORSYTH, ESQ. Edited, with Index, by F. J. COLLINSON, ESQ. Demy 8vo. Cloth. Rs. 5.

Ghose.—The Law of Mortgage in India. With the Transfer of Property Act and Notes. By RASHBEHARI GHOSE, M.A., D.L., Tagore Law Professor, 1876. Second Edition, Revised and Enlarged.

Grimley.—An Income - Tax Manual; being Act II of 1886. With Notes. By W. H. GRIMLEY, B. A., C. S., Commissioner of Income-Tax, Bengal. Royal 8vo. Rs. 3-8; Interleaved, Rs. 4.

MANUAL OF THE REVENUE SALE LAW AND CERTIFICATE Procedure of Lower Bengal, including the Acts on the Subject and Selections from the Rules and Circular Orders of the Board of Revenue. With Notes. By W. H. GRIMLEY, B.A., C. S. 8vo. Rs. 5-8; Interleaved, Rs. 6.

Henderson.—The Law of Intestate and Testamentary Succession in India; including the Indian Succession Act (X of 1865), with a Commentary; and the Parsee Succession Act (XXI of 1865), the Hindu Wills Act (XXI of 1870), the Probate and Administration Act, etc. With Notes and Cross References. By GILBERT S. HENDERSON, ESQ., M.A., Barrister-at-Law, and Advocate of the High Court at Calcutta. Royal 8vo., Cloth. Rs. 16.

Indian Emigration Act; with Orders by the Lieutenant-Governor of Bengal; Forms by Government of Bengal; Resolution of the Government of India; Resolution of the Government of Assam; Rules made by the Chief Commissioner of Assam; and Orders by the Lieutenant-Governor, N.-W. P. Interpaged with blank pages for notes. Crown 8vo. Rs. 2-4; cash 2.

Jolly.—The Hindu Law of Inheritance, Partition, and Adoption according to the Smritis. By Prof. JULIUS JOLLY, of Wurtzburg (Tagore Law Lectures, 1883). Royal 8vo. Rs. 10.

Lyon.—Medical Jurisprudence for India. By J B. LYON, F.C.S., F.C., Brigade-Surgeon, Professor of Medical Jurisprudence, Grant Medical College, Bombay. The Legal Matter revised by J. D. Inverarity, Barrister-at-Law. Illustrated. 8vo.

[*In the Press.*

MacEwen.—The Practice of the Presidency Court of Small Causes of Calcutta under the Presidency Small Cause Courts Act (XV of 1882). With Notes and an Appendix. By R. S. T. MACEWEN, ESQ., of Lincoln's Inn, Barrister-at-Law, one of the Judges of the Presidency Court of Small Causes of Calcutta. Thick 8vo. Rs. 11; cash 10.

O'Kinealy.—The Code of Civil Procedure, Act XIV of 1882. With Notes, Appendices, &c. By the Hon'ble J. O'KINEALY. Third Edition. Royal 8vo.

O'Kinealy.—THE INDIAN PENAL CODE; being Act XLV of 1860, and other Laws and Acts of Parliament relating to the Criminal Courts of India; containing Rulings on points of Procedure and Decisions of the High Court of Calcutta. Third Edition. By the Hon'ble J. O'KINEALY. Rl. 8vo. Rs. 12. [1886.

Pocket Penal, Criminal Procedure, and Police Codes, also the Whipping Act and the Railway Servants' Act; being Acts XLV of 1860 (with Amendments), X of 1882, V of 1861, VI of 1864, and XXXI of 1867. With a General Index. Fcap. 8vo. Cloth. Rs. 4.

Pocket (The) Code of Civil Law. Containing the Civil Procedure Code (Act XIV of 1882); The Court-Fees Act (VII of 1870); The Evidence Act (I of 1872); The Specific Relief Act (I of 1877); The Registration Act (III of 1877); The Limitation Act (XV of 1877); The Stamp Act (I of 1879). With Supplement containing the Amending Act of 1888. With a General Index Fcap 8vo. Cloth. Rs. 4.

Phillips.—MANUAL OF INDIAN CRIMINAL LAW; being the Penal Code, Criminal Procedure Code, Evidence, Whipping, General Clauses, Police, Cattle-Trespass, Extradition Acts. With Penal Clauses of Legal Practitioners' Act, Registration, Arms, Stamp, &c., Acts. Fully Annotated. and containing all applicable Rulings of all High Courts arranged under the appropriate Sections up to date; also Circular Orders and Notifications. By H. A. D. PHILLIPS, C. S. Second Edition. Thick crown 8vo. Rs. 10.

MANUAL OF REVENUE AND COLLECTORATE LAW. With Important Rulings and Annotations. By H. A. D. PHILLIPS, Bengal Civil Service. Crown 8vo. Cloth. Rs. 10. [1884.

CONTENTS:—Alluvion and Diluvion, Certificate, Cesses, Road and Public Works, Collectors, Assistant Collectors, Drainage, Embankment, Evidence, Excise, Lakhiraj Grants and Service Tenures, and Land Acquisition, Land Registration, Legal Practitioners, License Tax, Limitation, Opium, Partition, Public Demands Recovery, Putni Sales, Registration, Revenue Sales, Salt, Settlement, Stamps, Survey, and Wards.

Phillips.—Comparative Criminal Jurisprudence. Showing the Law, Procedure, and Case-Law of other Countries, arranged under the corresponding sections of the Indian Codes. By H. A. D. PHILLIPS, B. C. S. Vol. I.—Crimes and Punishments. Vol. II.—Procedure and Police. [*In the Press.*

Phillips.—OUR ADMINISTRATION OF INDIA. An Account of the Constitution and Working of the Civil Departments of the Indian Government, with special reference to the work and duties of a District Officer in Bengal. By H. A. D. PHILLIPS, C. S.. Author of "Manual of Indian Criminal Law," "Manual of Revenue and Collectorate Law." Crown 8vo. Rs. 4-4.

Phillips.—The Law relating to the Land Tenures of Lower Bengal. *Tagore Law Lectures.* 1875. By ARTHUR PHILLIPS, Esq. Royal 8vo. Cloth. Rs. 10.

Prinsep.—Code of Criminal Procedure (Act X of 1882), and other Laws and Rules of Practice relating to Procedure in the Criminal Courts of British India. With Notes. By H. T. PRINSEP. Eighth Edition. Royal 8vo. Rs. 12. [1887.

Regulations of the Bengal Code.—A Selection intended chiefly for the use of Candidates for appointments in the Judicial and Revenue Departments. Royal 8vo. Stitched. Rs. 8.

CONTENTS:—Regulations: 1793—I, II, VIII, X, XI, XIV, XIX, XXXVII, XXXVIII, XLIV, XLVIII, L. 1794—III. 1795—I, II, LI. 1798—I. 1799—VII. 1800—VIII, X. 1801—I. 1803—XXV, XXVII. 1804—V, X. 1806—XVII. 1807—VII. 1808—IV. 1814—XIX. 1817—V, XII, XX. 1818—III. 1819—I, II, VI, VIII. 1820—I. 1822—VI, VII. 1824—IX. 1825—IX, XI, XX. 1828—III, VII. 1833—IX.

Siromani.—A Commentary on Hindu Law of Inheritance, Succession, Partition, Adoption, Marriage, Stridhan, and Testamentary Disposition. By Pundit JOGENDRO NATH SMARTO SIROMANI (BHATTACHARJE), M.A., B.L. 8vo. Cloth. Rs. 12.

Sutherland.—The Digest of Indian Law Reports: a Compendium of the Rulings of the High Court of Calcutta from 1862 and of the Privy Council from 1831 to 1876. By D. SUTHERLAND, Esq., Barrister-at-Law. Impl. 8vo. Rs. 16. Vol. II, 1776 to 1881. Rs. 6.

THE INDIAN CONTRACT ACT (IX of 1872) and the Specific Relief Act (I of 1877). With a Full Commentary. By D. SUTHERLAND, Esq. Second Edition. Royal 8vo. Cloth. Rs. 5.

Toynbee.—The Village Chaukidari Manual; being Act VI, B. C., of 1870, as amended by Acts I, B.C., of 1871 and 1886. With Notes, Appendices, &c. By G. TOYNBEE, C.S., Magistrate of Hooghly. Crown 8vo. Cloth. Re. 1.

TAGORE LAW LECTURES.

The Hindu Law.—Being a Treatise on the Law administered exclusively to Hindus by the British Courts in India. (1870 and 1871.) By HERBERT COWELL. Royal 8vo., 2 vols., cloth, Rs. 12 and 8.

History and Constitution of the Courts and Legislative. Authorities. (1884.) By HERBERT COWELL. New Edition. (1884). Demy 8vo. Rs. 6.

Mahomedan Law.—By SHAMA CHURN SIRCAR. Digest of Laws according to Sunni Code, Rs. 9. (1873.) Sunni Code in part and Immayah Code Rs. 9, (1874.)

The Law relating to the Land Tenures of Lower Bengal.—(1875.) By ARTHUR PHILLIPS. Rs. 10.

The Law relating to Mortgage in India.—Including the Transfer of Property. (1876). Second Edition. By RASH BEHARI GHOSE. M.A., D.L.

The Law relating to Minors in Bengal.—(1877). By E. J. TREVELYAN. Royal 8vo., cloth. Rs. 10.

The Hindu Law of Marriage and Stridhana.—(1878). By GOOROO DOSS BANERJEE. Royal 8vo. Rs. 10.

The Law relating to the Hindu Widow.—By TRAILOKYANATH MITTRA, M. A., D.L. Rs. 10. (1879).

The Principles of the Hindu Law of Inheritance.—By RAJCOOMAR SARVDHICARI, B.L. Rs. 16. (1880).

The Hindu Law of Inheritance, Partition, and Adoption. according to the Smritis. By Dr. JULIUS JOLLY (1883.) Rs. 10.

The Law relating to Gifts, Trusts, and Testamentary. Disposition among the Mahomedans. By SYED AMEER ALI. (1884.) Rs. 12.

THACKER, SPINK AND CO., CALCUTTA.

The Fauna of British India.—Including Ceylon and Burma. Published under the authority of the Secretary of State for India. Edited by W. T. BLANFORD, F. R. S., and Illustrated.

Part I, Mammalia. By W. T. BLANFORD, F. R. S. Half vol., pp. 1, XII, 1—250 and 71 woodcuts. Price, Rs. 7-8.

A History of the Native States of India. Vol. I. Gwalior. By SURENDRA NATH ROY, B. A. B. L., Rl. 8vo. Rs. 10.

India in 1887.—As seen by ROBERT WALLACE, Professor of Agriculture and Rural Economy in the University of Edinburgh. 8vo. Rs. 13.

Chapters on Cattle, Milk, Horses, Buffaloes, Mules, Sheeps, Goats, Pigs—Soils, Native Implements, Irrigation, Crops, Currency or Silver Question, Grasses and Grass Lands, Forestry, Chemistry Veterinary Science, a Department of Agriculture. 105 Photo Tints and other illustrations and 3 Maps.

A few plain Truths about India.—By SIR RICHARD GARTH, Q.C. Price, Re. 1.

Statement of the Uncovenanted Civil Service in India, prepared by the Committee of the Uncovenanted Civil Service Association, London, on behalf of the Service. 8vo. Sewed. As. 8.

The Grammar of Indian Finance 1874-75 to 1883-84. By T. HESKETH BIGGS, F.S.S., Financial Department of the Government of India. 8vo. Re. 1-14. Supplement 1883-84 to 1886-87. Re. 1-8.

Annals of Rural Bengal. By W. W. HUNTER, C.I.E., LL.D. 8vo. Rs. 9.

Sketchy Memories of Eton 1866-1872. By "MAC." Fcap. 8vo. Re. 1.

The Highlands of India. Vol. II. Being a Chronicle of Field Sports and Travel in India. With 32 full page and 201 Text Illustrations, Diagrams, &c. By General D. J. F. NEWALL, R. A. 8vo. Rs. 15-12.

CONTENTS:—Cashmere, The Kohisthan of the Punjab, Simla and the Basins of the Sutlej and Giri, The Basins of the Jumna and Ganges, Gurhwal and Kumaon, Nepal and the Basins of the Karnali, Gunduk and Cosi, Darjeeling and Sikkim, The Khasia Hills, The Southern Highlands, Maharashtra and Central India, Rajasthan.

Vol. I. The Highlands of India Strategitically considered with special reference to their Colonization as Reserve Circles. With Map, Diagrams, and Illustrations. By General D. J. F. NEWALL, R. A. Rs. 15-12.
